D1518265

★ ★ ★ ★ ★ ★ ★

THE POLITICS OF PARTICIPATION IN

POVERTY

★ ★ ★ ★ ★ ★ ★ ★ ★ ★ ★ ★ ★ ★

THE POLITICS OF
PARTICIPATION IN
POVERTY

★ ★ ★ ★ ★ ★ ★ ★ ★ ★ ★ ★ ★

UNIVERSITY OF CALIFORNIA PRESS

★ ★ ★ ★ ★ ★ ★ ★ ★ ★ ★ ★ ★ ★

A CASE STUDY OF THE BOARD OF THE
ECONOMIC AND YOUTH OPPORTUNITIES
AGENCY OF GREATER LOS ANGELES

BY DALE ROGERS MARSHALL

★ ★ ★ ★ ★ ★ ★ ★ ★ ★ ★ ★ ★

BERKELEY · LOS ANGELES · LONDON   1971

☆ ☆ ☆ ☆ ☆ ☆ ☆ ☆ ☆ ☆ ☆ ☆

UNIVERSITY OF CALIFORNIA PRESS · BERKELEY AND LOS ANGELES, CALIFORNIA

UNIVERSITY OF CALIFORNIA PRESS, LIMITED · · · · LONDON, ENGLAND

COPYRIGHT © 1971 BY THE REGENTS OF THE UNIVERSITY OF CALIFORNIA

ISBN: 0-520-01741-2 · LIBRARY OF CONGRESS CATALOG CARD NUMBER: 79-121192

PRINTED IN THE UNITED STATES OF AMERICA · DESIGNED BY DAVE COMSTOCK

☆ ☆ ☆ ☆ ☆ ☆ ☆ ☆ ☆ ☆ ☆

TO JESSICA WOOD LANGSTON
1880–1967
WHO WOULD BE GLAD HER GRANDDAUGHTER
HAS COMPLETED THE PROJECT

Acknowledgments

I wish to thank the board members and staff of the Economic and Youth Opportunities Agency of Greater Los Angeles for their invaluable help in this project. Though facing an endless stream of people doing studies, they received me with a friendliness and frankness that made 1968 a memorable year of on-the-job training.

I would also like to thank Professors John C. Ries, Harry M. Scoble, Howard Elinson, Peter Orleans, Dwaine Marvick, Richard Longaker, and Charles Nixon. All helped to show that faculty members can be unpretentious, concerned human beings and that aloofness to current problems is not an essential attribute of academicians. In particular I want to thank Professor John C. Bollens, whose encouraging response to a phone call from an unknown housewife in 1965 got me back to school in the first place.

Finally, it is a pleasure to acknowledge the unique support given by Donald J. Marshall and Jessica and Cynthia Marshall.

Contents

Tables

I: THE SETTING
★ ★ ★ ★ ★ ★ ★

1. Introduction

On August 20, 1964, the United States Congress passed the Economic Opportunity Act with the stated goal of mobilizing the human and financial resources of the country to combat poverty. The Act states that community action programs are to be "developed, conducted, and administered with the maximum feasible participation of residents of the areas and members of the groups served."[1] Owing to this maximum feasible participation clause, representatives of the poor have been added to the local governing boards of community action agencies (CAAs) throughout the country.[2] In a unique social experiment, people from widely divergent economic and social levels are sitting together as equal voting members on more than a thousand boards of directors of community action agencies responsible for administering the war on poverty at the local level.

On the Los Angeles CAA board, for example, there is a twice-divorced woman with six children who is on welfare and had never been an active member of any organization until she was elected to the board. One of her fellow board members is a highly successful businessman who had been an officer of many prominent community service organizations in Los Angeles and a board member of leading private corporations. Another board member is a woman who had never registered to vote until the year she joined the board. On the same board sits an active political campaign worker who serves as an aide to an elected official. There is a man from the schools with a doctorate in education who ordinarily would not have to listen to complaints about the schools from a parent who had finished only the eighth grade; but when that parent is on the board, his vote on the school proposal may be of interest. It is hard to imagine any other

organizational setting prior to the 1960s in which such diverse people
would come into contact as peers.

The addition of poor people to CAA boards is an apparent
change in participation patterns. Generally, poor people have a low
level of participation in organizations and politics.[3] But the Economic Opportunity Act has meant that representatives of the poor
become at least formal participants at the top level of an organization
making public policy. What happens when representatives of the low
socioeconomic class that is characterized by little participation are
designated as participants in an organization to which they would not
ordinarily have access? What happens when such diverse people are
on the same decision-making board?

This study of local political participation analyzes the change
in participation patterns. It focuses on what happens when representatives of the poor become members of the board of one CAA, the
Economic and Youth Opportunities Agency of Greater Los Angeles
(EYOA). This organization is the major CAA in Los Angeles
County; it handles more than $125 million in federal funds and
serves an area of almost 4,000 square miles, including approximately
250,000 poverty-level families.[4] The board of EYOA is responsible
for planning, conducting, and evaluating the poverty program in
most of Los Angeles County. For example, it screens proposals from
community groups wishing to obtain poverty funds for such programs
as Head Start, presents a package of approved proposals to Washington, and then subcontracts with the local groups to run those programs funded by the federal government.

THE APPROACH

The present research analyzes how the board of the Economic
and Youth Opportunities Agency has functioned since community
representatives were added.[5] By focusing on the interaction between
the poverty members and the other members of the board, it investi-
gates the process rather than the product. It asks two central questions: how much power do the poverty representatives really have on
the board, and what effect does the board have on the attitudes of the
members? The board process is viewed in terms of both co-optation
(who is using whom)[6] and socialization (who is learning what).[7]

Participation of the poor in the war on poverty is pertinent to
the debate in the social sciences on the general topic of political par-

ticipation. Some social scientists are not worried about the current participation patterns; their position is that low participation by poor people is consistent with functioning democracy since both active and passive roles are needed and minimal surveillance by the public is enough.[8] Other social scientists argue for changes in participation patterns. They see the relationship of low income to low participation as undesirable because it results in differential access to political power.[9] They argue for the involvement of larger numbers of people. This position is subject to many types of criticism. Some say it is dangerous to increase the participation of low socioeconomic groups because they tend to be activated by demagogues and will pose a threat to a liberal political system.[10] Others question the feasibility of involving the poor—whether it can be done with any success—or the effectiveness of various techniques being used to increase participation.[11]

While scholars ponder the desirability and feasibility of changing participation patterns, the poverty program provides numerous opportunities for studying the questions in a concrete way.[12] Studies of the participation in poverty programs can add to our extremely limited knowledge about the conditions under which persons who feel politically deprived shift from withdrawal to participation, and the conditions under which they choose to accept rather than to try to overthrow the existing political system.[13]

Representatives of the poor have actually been added to the poverty boards, and we do not even know what effect this inclusion has had on the participants. To what extent does board membership represent a change in participation by the community representatives? If it is a change, why did they become participants? How much do they actually participate? Has membership increased their support for CAA and the war on poverty? Has it increased their belief in their own efficacy and strengthened their affection for the political system? Has it effected their participation in politics and organizations? These are some of the questions we shall consider.[14]

This study analyses the changes in attitude of both the community representatives and the other board members. One might ask why the attitudes of the other board members are relevant to a study concerned with changes in participation by poor people; after all, the other board members presumably have already been socialized into the political system, that is, they already exhibit a high level of organizational and political participation. Yet the problem of the low participation of poor people is here presumed to be related both to the behavior of the poor and to the behavior of the high participators. For example, the attitudes of the community representatives on the EYOA board undoubtedly will be influenced by the attitudes of the other board members. How often do the experienced members treat the inexperienced members as inferiors by making remarks such as "I don't think you can possibly understand the situation"? And the attitudes of the community representatives will undoubtedly influence the attitude of the other board members toward them, which will in turn influence the community representatives. This study of changes in participation by poor people will therefore consider the effect of board membership on both the poor and the other members of the board. The changes in attitude that take place will be viewed as involving interaction among all the board members.

In addition to having implications for questions about political participation patterns, this study is relevant to the field of adult socialization[15] and to the increasing number of situations in which the poor are included in groups previously closed to them and there is a power differential in the interaction between the poor and the other members.[16] Furthermore, the study of CAAs helps draw attention to the importance of new governmental phenomena such as the plethora of local authorities involved in urban renewal, model cities programs, and the war on poverty, which do not fit into the traditional categories and which merit more attention from political scientists. In addition, this study should provide new insights into the local politics of Los Angeles.[17] EYOA offers a smaller decision-making arena which reflects the metropolis's patterns of influence and institutional relationships and is thus a valuable research setting for discovering the forces most relevant to politics in Los Angeles.[18]

RESEARCH PROCEDURES

The present research is based on interviews with board members, the observation of board meetings and committee meetings, and the examination of written information about the board. I conducted interviews with thirty-two board members. They were the twenty-five board members as of January 1968[19] and the seven new community representatives who were elected in March 1968. The major part of the interviewing was done between February and June of 1968.[20]

The interviews were unstructured but focused. A separate interview checklist was developed for each type of member—the newly elected community representatives, the originally elected community representatives, and the agency representatives.[21] The checklists were used to elicit comparable types of information from all the respondents—information on their recruitment, the functioning of the board, and changes in their own attitudes—but the actual interviews did not follow a set pattern and the questions were unstructured. Structured questions may be more efficient, but they may also eliminate valuable responses, especially in an exploratory study. The strength of field studies is their ability to discover significant variables and relationships that might not be revealed by a prematurely rigid approach.[22] The goal in the interviews was to gain a thorough understanding of how the subjects themselves saw the board. The interviewer was supportive rather than provocative, since further contact with the subjects during observation of board meetings was desired. The interviews took place in offices or homes and were between a half hour to two and a half hours long.

Access did not prove to be difficult. Since the interviewer was introduced at a board meeting and had been attending meetings, most subjects had seen the interviewer prior to the interview. The subjects were guaranteed anonymity, which posed a serious difficulty in the reporting of the results.[23] Many times a generalization cannot be supported by citing specific interview results because the quote or the paraphrase would reveal the identity of the source. In such instances, supporting data have been omitted or certain details slightly modified to conceal identities.[24]

The interviews were taped to allow closer analysis of the attitudes revealed by the respondents. If the study had attempted to find out why certain decisions were made, the possible loss of frankness about inside details might have outweighed the advantages of having a transcript. But since the prime interest was in discovering the attitudes of the board members, the opportunity to capture their personal style in transcripts seemed worth the risk.[25]

It is hard to evaluate the frankness of respondents or how responses would have varied on a different day with another interviewer, but most respondents appeared candid, as indicated by their willingness to answer questions about their attitudes toward other board members. It was anticipated that agency representatives would tend to talk officially rather than as individuals, but in fact, most were franker than expected and seemed to enjoy the chance to talk anonymously to someone not involved with the war on poverty.[26] Several subjects, especially the agency representatives, at first worded their answers carefully, because of the presence of a tape recorder. But most subjects quickly became more informal, perhaps because the interviewer intentionally used casual language and made personal comments. As a further check against distortion owing to the presence of the tape recorder, near the end of the interview the recorder was openly turned off and the conversation purposely continued. Little if any change in tone was noticed. Several agency respondents followed sensitive revelations with remarks such as "this does not go in your report," or "you are sure you won't quote me by name?" Only one asked that the tape recorder be turned off before commenting negatively on certain board members (it was turned off).

To expedite the interviews, the agency representatives were asked to fill out a brief socioeconomic questionnaire after the interview and mail it to the interviewer.[27] The items on the questionnaire were put orally to the community representatives during their interviews. This decision was made because the middle-class bias in standard socioeconomic questions about parents and work history can be very insulting. Further, since the life histories of the community representatives were of particular interest, it seemed worthwhile to talk about them in detail.

The objection may be raised that single interviews cannot reveal what the board members were learning. It was possible to overcome this objection in the case of the seven new community representatives; they were interviewed in March before they had met with the board and were then reinterviewed in September after they had been on the board for six months.[28] But in defense of retrospective recall it must be noted that the subjectivity of the respondents' comments on their own learning does not mean that the comments lack value. How people think they have changed can be just as important as a more objective measure of how they have actually changed. What people think they have learned may be very significant in how they consequently behave and influence other people.[29]

A second major source of data for this study was participant observation of board meetings and committee meetings between January and September 1968.[30] The field observation provided a valuable supplement to the data gained by interviews. It provided the opportunity to compare what appeared to the observer to be happening with what the subjects said was happening; it suggested incongruities and connections to pursue.[31] Written information on EYOA provided a third source of data; it included board and committee minutes, the files of some staff members, press releases and newspaper coverage, and testimony at congressional hearings on the war on poverty.

The interpretation of the three main sources of data was necessarily subjective. Even in transcribing the taped interviews, questions of interpretation crept in. Words are not always spoken clearly and meanings are less clear. Attempts to classify nonstructured answers involve more judgments. Just as Mailer called his description of the march on the Pentagon both history as the novel and the novel as history,[32] the social scientist must recognize that his work may be called research as fiction or fiction as research.[33] Yet there is value in attempting to look at a phenomenon from the outside, and to base interpretation on facts that are not infinitely malleable. As a check on the author's interpretation, the respondents were given parts of the first draft of this analysis.[34] Their comments proved very helpful and led to numerous revisions which should increase the reliability of the findings.

CHAPTER FORMAT

Before discussing the findings on the effects of adding community representatives to EYOA, several preliminary matters must be covered. The rest of this chapter briefly reviews the major features of the war on poverty. Chapter 2 discusses the war on poverty in the Los Angeles area. A brief description is given of Los Angeles politics and the creation of EYOA. The structure and program of EYOA are compared with other community action agencies.

The findings reported in chapters 3 through 6 must be considered against this setting. The first step in answering questions about what happens when community representatives are added to the board is describing the community representatives and the other board members. How did they get on the board and what are they like? This forms the content of chapter 3. Chapter 4 discusses how the board functions, with emphasis on determining how much power the community representatives have on the board. Both chapters 5 and 6 focus on what effect the board has on the attitudes of the members—what are their attitudes toward EYOA, and community representatives, and politics? What changes took place in their attitudes? Chapter 5 is based on the retrospective recall of the eight original community representatives and the other board members. Chapter 6 concentrates on the socialization of the seven newly elected community representatives who were interviewed before they served on the board and then reinterviewed after being on the board for six months. The concluding chapter summarizes the main themes and focuses on the implications of the findings for both theory and policy.

THE WAR ON POVERTY

Studies of the political forces behind the Economic Opportunity Act of 1964 suggest that it was developed by the executive branch partly to help win the election that year. It was skillfully drafted to build support among the agencies and external clientele and was passed by a coalition of diverse forces.[35] The final legislation bore the marks of the compromises necessary to obtain that support. The original proposal, as developed by the Council of Economic Advisors and the Bureau of the Budget, focused on a community action program that would provide general purpose grants to umbrella community organizations in various localities. But in the maneuvering to gain agreement this focus was abandoned and a package of diverse proposals was developed to be broad and spectacular, and to satisfy as many of the interested constituencies as possible. The community action program became Title II in a total of seven titles, each providing for distinct types of programs. Yet today there is general agreement that the community action program was the only major innovation in the bill and was an innovation of "surpassing importance."[36] Title II specified that community action programs could be administered by either a public or a private nonprofit agency but that they must be "developed, conducted, and administered with the maximum feasible participation of residents of the areas and members of the groups served."[37]

Although there is continuing debate over how the concept of maximum feasible participation was formulated, it is clear that the concept meant different things to different people involved in developing the poverty proposal.[38] People worked together to draft the proposal and get it passed without realizing the incompatibility of their interpretations. But when the community action programs were implemented, the conflict between the interpretations became clear. The discrepancy was basically between the view that community action programs should help the poor adapt to the system and the view that they should modify the system by increasing the power of the poor to change that system.[39] The former assumed a paternalistic and consensus model of social change, the latter a democratic or participatory and conflict model of social change.[40]

The guidelines for community action programs developed by the Office of Economic Opportunity did not resolve the discrepancy; they were contradictory and vague. The structure of CAA boards and the criteria for maximum feasible participation were not specified.[41] Public controversy emerged over the implementation of the guidelines between advocates of organizing the poor and others such as mayors who felt that the organized poor could pose a threat.[42]

In 1966 the Economic Opportunity Act was amended to specify criteria for involving the poor. The poor, it said, should comprise at least a third of the CAA board's membership and representatives of the poor should live in the area they represent and be selected by "the residents in areas of concentration of poverty, with special emphasis on participation by the residents of the area who are poor."[43] In 1966 Congress also cut back the amount of discretionary funds allotted to CAAs thus toning down the idea of organizing the poor. Funds for community action programs were earmarked for programs such as Head Start, which were considered safe because they did not emphasize organizing the poor.[44]

In 1967 the Green amendment continued the trend away from the conflict view of community action by stating that local governments have the responsibility for establishing community action agencies and that a third of the board members were to be public officials.[45] Thus in a move led by southern Democrats and acquiesced in by liberal Democrats and the White House, legislation that opponents referred to as the "bosses and boll weevil bill" gave control of local poverty programs to elective officials.[46] Local governments were, however, given the option of designating themselves the CAA or naming a public or private nonprofit agency as the CAA. Study of the effects of the Green amendments shows that massive takeovers of CAAs by local governments did not occur; most local governments redesignated existing CAAs but changes in board membership did increase the influence of public officials.[47]

Even though nationally the war on poverty shows a trend away from organizing the poor and the studies of the idea are often pessimistic,[48] proponents refuse to give up hope. They say that the issue of involving the poor in the political system has been raised in a more compelling way than ever before; "the seed has been planted, and the idea will not die out."[49] It is much too early to assess the accuracy of this position with any finality, but evaluation will require close consideration of the implementation of community action programs throughout the country.

The war on poverty in Los Angeles can provide useful data for judging the impact of participation by the poor. The next chapter describes the Los Angeles poverty program which provides the setting for this study of participation on the board of EYOA.

2. The Los Angeles Area as a Case Study

The war on poverty is seen in a different way when one's focus shifts from the national to the local scene. There are over a thousand community action agencies involved in administering the war on poverty in local communities. At this level national and local forces converge and the resulting poverty programs can only be understood in the light of this interaction. This chapter asks questions about the Los Angeles version of the war on poverty. How did the Los Angeles area implement the national guidelines discussed in the preceding chapter, and how does the Los Angeles CAA compare with other efforts?[1]

The well-worn generalizations about Los Angeles government and politics are supported by a review of how Los Angeles set up an organization to administer poverty programs. Both formally and informally Los Angeles's power structure is fragmented. Formally there is a division of authority among the city, county, and state governments. Within the city, authority is further divided between a weak mayor and a strong council and a plethora of independent boards and commissions.[2] The formal decentralization is not counteracted by informal centralization. The party organizations are very weak. Elections for local officials are nonpartisan, and civil service systems mean that effective patronage is almost nonexistent.[3] The absence of centralization and of hierarchy contributes to an apparent political vacuum in Los Angeles. Groups that aspire to power must search for it in a situation where no power seems to exist; the demands of civic organizations aften get "lost in the political maze of a decentralized system."[4]

The development of EYOA began in 1962 when its predecessor, the Youth Opportunities Board (YOB), was set up to receive grants from the President's Committee on Juvenile Delinquency. Owing to the political fragmentation of Los Angeles, the development of a social service program required coordination among the governmental jurisdictions involved. The county government, not the city, had jurisdiction over the health, probation, and welfare services in the city, so when the city wanted to have a voice in these services it had to work with the county.

Bollens has traced the details of how cooperation among the governmental jurisdictions shaped the Youth Opportunities Board.[5] After attending a Washington conference related to the President's Committee on Juvenile Delinquency in the spring of 1961, Karl Holton, who was head of the Probation Department of Los Angeles County, reported to the county supervisors that he would try to mobilize public and private local groups to develop a coordinated social services program. But no concrete plan developed out of the resulting meetings until January 1962, when Mayor Yorty's executive assistant, Robert Goe, proposed that the governmental agencies form a partnership under the Joint Powers Act, which made such action possible. This idea was accepted and in April 1962 a Joint Powers Agreement was signed by five governmental entities—the city, the county, the city and county schools, and the state.

The resulting Youth Opportunities Board was a public agency comparable to a special district. The five-man governing board was made up of a representative from each signatory body. It could receive and disburse funds and exercise any power common to the contracting parties. Its purpose was area-wide coordination and planning; some also viewed it as a stimulus for change within the existing governmental agencies. The fact that private agencies were not on the board supports the generalization that private welfare agencies in Los Angeles are of less significance than the public ones.[6]

The Youth Opportunities Board functioned for two years under grants from the President's Committee on Juvenile Delinquency and Youth Crime and from the Office of Manpower, Automation, and Training in the Department of Labor. While intended as a coordinating agency, it is debatable how much coordination occurred.

Marris and Rein entitle their section on YOB, "Los Angeles: All Against Coordination." They argue that "in practice, institutions remained stubbornly self-interested, and their formal endorsement of the project did not guarantee any commitment to its aims. The new agency merely provided another setting in which to deploy the struggle for power, and generated, not a self-sustaining process of reform, but a self-sustaining conflict over the control of reform."[7] Yet participants maintain that in spite of self-interest more coordination occurred than in the past so YOB was an improvement.

After the passage of the Economic Opportunity Act in 1964, the YOB submitted proposals to the Office of Economic Opportunity in the hope of becoming the central community action agency for Los Angeles. But at the same time a new private organization was formed, the Economic Opportunity Federation, which also aimed to become the Los Angeles community action agency. It had a fifteen-member board made up of six representatives from private agencies, five from the public agencies, and four members at large, including one representative from the Negro community and one from the Mexican-American community.[8] This organization was formed by those who felt that YOB was controlled by Mayor Yorty and was harmful to their interests. It had the support of the Welfare Planning Council and a number of Los Angeles congressmen, including Augustus Hawkins, Edward Roybal, James Roosevelt, and George Brown.[9]

The Office of Economic Opportunity told the two organizations that they must merge and include more representatives of the poor on the new board of directors to qualify as the CAA for Los Angeles. In the winter of 1965 an agreement along these lines was worked out; the board of directors of the new agency was to have ten representatives of governmental agencies, six from private agencies, and six community representatives. All that was needed was ratification by the governmental bodies. But in April, Mayor Yorty publicly announced his opposition to the merger on the grounds that it would put control of the new organization into the hands of people not elected by the taxpayers. Then a new private organization, the Community Anti-Poverty Committee, was formed in Congressman Hawkins' office with Reverend H. H. Brookins of the United Civil Rights Committee and Tony Rios of the Community Service Organization as cochairmen. Some of the people involved in this group had originally favored the merger but now they stressed the need for more representatives from the poor and opposed any organization in which governmental representatives would have a majority.

After the Watts riots in August 1965, Governor LeRoy Collins was sent to Los Angeles by President Johnson to solve the dispute. Seeing that a mutually agreeable solution was impossible, Collins decided that the best that could be achieved was a partial agreement. The solution was very similar to the merger agreement except that governmental representatives were given a majority; this was a concession to them. A second major change was that the community representatives were to be democratically selected and not subject to approval by the governmental powers. This change was a concession to the Community Anti-Poverty Committee but was unsatisfactory to it. Nevertheless, Collins informed Shriver that an agreement had been reached, which really meant that the governmental agencies and private agencies were ready to go along even though the Community Anti-Poverty Committee was not.[10]

THE STRUCTURE AND JURISDICTION OF EYOA

The community action agency of Los Angeles, named the Economic and Youth Opportunities Board of Greater Los Angeles and created in August 1965, was a special intergovernmental agency formed by a Joint Powers Agreement signed by the city, the county, and the city and county schools. These agencies are referred to as the joint powers. The public character of EYOA differentiates it from most other CAAs, which are private nonprofit organizations.[11]

In September 1965, EYOA had twenty-five members on the Board of Directors. The twenty-three voting members included: (1) Twelve members from the joint powers with unlimited terms: three appointed by the County Board of Supervisors; three from the county schools; three appointed by the Mayor of the City of Los Angeles and approved by the City Council; three appointed by the Board of Education of the Los Angeles City Schools. (2) Four private agency representatives with unlimited terms: one from United Way; one from the AFL-CIO; one from the Welfare Planning Council; one from the Los Angeles County Federation of Coordinating Councils. (3) Seven community representatives democratically selected for two year terms: four selected from city territory, and three selected from the county territory outside the city. The city was to appoint the former, the county to appoint the latter. The two nonvoting members were from the Chamber of Commerce and the League of California Cities.[12]

Since 1965 the membership of the board has been changed to comply with congressional amendments to the Economic Opportunity Act. In the spring of 1967 an additional community representative was added so that the poor would constitute a third of the board. In July 1968 major changes were made in response to the Green amendment. The number of public agency representatives was cut from twelve to eight to comply with the requirement that a third of the board consist of public representatives. And the number of private agency representatives was increased from four to eight. The four new voting members were the Chamber of Commerce, the League of California Cities, an Oriental organization, and an Indian organization.[13]

EYOA's board is one of the smaller ones in the country[14] and has the minimum number of community representatives allowable. Some boards, such as those in San Francisco, New York, and Oakland have a majority of community representatives.[15] EYOA's method of selecting the community representatives is also different from procedures used in other CAAs, but since the selection system is particularly important for the present study of EYOA it is treated separately later in this chapter.

Unlike many boards, the EYOA board does not have an executive committee. The committee structure has changed several times but there have been three important standing committees concerned with program planning, program management, and personnel. In addition, there have been several important ad hoc committees, the most permanent being the election committee. Appointments to the committees are formally made by the chairman of the board, but suggestions from the executive staff are usually followed. The policy has been to have equal representation from the three types of board members—public, private, and community—on each committee.

EYOA is one of the few CAAs in the country which does not provide for any kind of neighborhood councils.[16] The Economic Opportunity Act encourages the formation of such councils[17] and EYOA spent over a year in planning for them, but the expected funds from the Office of Economic Opportunity did not materialize and plans for the Economic Opportunity Area Councils were dropped. The official explanation is that the Office for Economic Opportunity needed the funds to cover the additional administrative costs of four new CAAs created in Los Angeles County.[18] The decision to stop the formation of area councils, however, is still a major subject of debate. Some feel that EYOA could have gone ahead without funds and that the failure to do so indicates that the joint powers and the executive director did not really want communities to be organized.

The jurisdiction of EYOA originally covered all the territory in Los Angeles County. But since 1967, the Office of Economic Opportunity has recognized four other CAAs in the county, located in Long Beach, Compton, East Los Angeles, and Pasadena. The ostensible purpose was to bring CAAs closer to the community, but undoubtedly pressures from interested congressmen played a part. Similar pressures for the proliferation of CAAs in metropolitan areas are apparently increasing.[19]

PURPOSES AND OPERATION OF EYOA

The Senate study of CAAs classifies them according to whether their main purpose is to provide services or to change institutions. Using these categories EYOA would clearly fall into the first one, as do most of the CAAs in the nation.[20] The purpose mentioned most often in EYOA publications and in the interviews is service. The goal is to provide service and involve people so that they can improve their lives.

EYOA is an organization that, to use Rossi and Dentler's phrase, was created from the top down. Correspondingly, it concentrates on the "downtown road" to poverty programs, on getting cooperation from the established agencies.[21] And in this it is similar to other CAAs. A study by the Advisory Commission on Intergovernmental Relations found that more than half, and perhaps as much as two-thirds, of the community action funds are channeled to the established agencies that serve as delegate agencies for the CAAs.[22] Originally EYOA operated some programs itself, but in 1966, like most other CAAs, it divested control of these programs to delegate agencies. Since that time EYOA has administered the war on poverty by channeling federal funds to delegate agencies that actually run the programs. These include manpower, education, neighborhood development, and law and delinquency programs.

Many staff members of EYOA indicate that since the 1966

divestiture of operating programs EYOA has become increasingly bureaucratic and institutionalized. The emphasis has been on administration rather than innovation. Procedures have been stressed; planning and research have been drastically de-emphasized. Instead, the focus has been on accounting and monitoring programs. EYOA is apparently following a typical organizational pattern of routinization.[23] The first executive director saw this as regrettable but inevitable when an organization is responsible for the handling of large sums of money.[24] Many people connected with EYOA deny that it was inevitable and blame a lack of strong leadership and a fear of conflict. They suggest that since institutionalization has occurred, EYOA is no longer where the action is; other programs are now in the spotlight.[25]

EYOA has been relatively free of scandal and major upheavals. In other cities CAAs have disbanded or been thrown into chaos by successive takeovers by different factions.[26] But EYOA has operated with the same basic structure and balance of power since its inception. One factor in this stability was the willingness of the first executive director, Joe Maldonado, to avoid disturbing the balance. He was the one candidate for the position of executive director of YOB on whom all the signatory parties could agree and was chosen for this reason. A Mexican-American with a background in social work in Los Angeles, he was executive director of the Council of Social Planning for Alameda County and participated in Oakland's Interagency Project funded by the Ford Foundation, before returning to Los Angeles in 1964 to direct a project run by YOB. His ethnic background and social work experience in political settings and in Los Angeles made him attractive to the joint powers. He remained an executive director longer than almost any other community action program director in the country, resigning in August 1968. It was only in the last year that any signs of infighting about the executive director appeared among the signatory parties. This hostility, plus trends within the Office of Economic Opportunity and the national political situation may have helped convince him that it was time to resign.[27]

SELECTION OF COMMUNITY REPRESENTATIVES

The Joint Powers Agreement that set up EYOA required the democratic selection of the community representatives rather than selection by the public agencies. Until 1966 some CAAs, most notably Chicago, had poverty representatives selected by officials.[28] After 1966 all poverty representatives had to be selected democratically, but many different selection methods fit this criteria. Los Angeles used a direct general election. A more prevalent method is indirect selection, whereby community representatives are chosen by elected neighborhood councils, as in Philadelphia, or community representatives are chosen at community meetings attended by delegates of organizations in that area, as in New York.[29] Los Angeles is the only major metropolitan area in which the electorate votes directly for the community representatives to sit on the CAA board.

The Los Angeles election did not focus on poverty pockets alone; instead it focused on poverty-level people no matter where they lived within EYOA's jurisdiction. The Office of Economic Opportunity guidelines permit poverty representatives to be selected by all the residents in a poverty area; the guidelines do not require that the selection be made only by poor people.[30] But in Los Angeles one of the first decisions made about the election was that only poor people could vote (the poor being defined as those with a family income of less than $4,000 regardless of the number of dependents) and that all poor people in the vast area covered by EYOA would be eligible to vote. It was also decided that all the candidates for election must be poor, even though the Office of Economic Opportunity guidelines say that representatives of the poor do not need to be poor themselves.[31]

Los Angeles is the only major metropolitan CAA that made all poverty-level people eligible to vote no matter where they lived within the metropolitan area. For example, Hartford, Atlanta, New York, Philadelphia, Chester, and Syracuse made residence in specific poverty areas plus income the criteria for eligibility. Why did Los Angeles make the decision it did? EYOA staff members say the decision was fairer and more democratic than making area the criterion because in Los Angeles poverty families are widely dispersed; they say that 53 percent of the people with incomes of $4,000 or less live outside the poverty areas.[32] The joint powers wanted income to be the criterion in order to prove they were not trying to take the election away from the poor. Others indicate, however, that the joint powers wanted income to be the criterion since this would make the election districts very large and would prevent representatives from developing real ties with their constituents and gaining a power base.[33]

Another characteristic of the Los Angeles election was that it involved single-member election districts. The whole city territory was divided into four election districts and the county territory outside the city was divided into three districts in the first election and four in the second. The county health districts formed the basis of the election districts, but various changes were made to separate city from county and to attempt to equalize the number of poor people in districts. Most of the public controversy surrounding the first election centered on charges that the boundaries were gerrymandered; few questioned the other aspects of the election design described above.[34]

Certain aspects of Los Angeles' first election were changed in the second election held two years later. In the first election no registration campaign was carried out, but in the second, registration was used primarily as a person-to-person get out the vote technique. (It was possible to vote even if one had not registered in advance.) In the second election all voters who registered two weeks before the election were supposed to receive a ballot in the mail which they could return in the same manner. In the first election, voting took place in public schools. In the second election, those who did not choose to vote by mail were to vote at Head Start centers.

Fifty-six candidates ran for seven community representative positions in the first election. About 6,000 people signed nominating petitions, but the total number of votes cast was 2,689.[35] This was a turnout of less than a 1 percent, and it made the Philadelphia turnout of 12,589, or 2 percent, look large and the Hartford turnout of 6 percent tremendous.[36] A breakdown of the vote in Los Angeles is shown in table 1. The largest turnouts were in areas generally thought of as poverty areas, districts II (East Los Angeles County), V (East Los Angeles City), and VI (Watts). They were also the areas where the door-to-door get out the vote campaign was carried on. The smallest turnouts were in areas not usually identified with poverty: IV (San Fernando Valley and West Los Angeles), I (Pasadena, Glendale), and III (Malibu, Palos Verdes, and many other areas). And even though district III had twice as many eligible voters as any other district, its turnout was smaller than that of five other districts.

In the second EYOA election fewer candidates, only thirty-six, ran for the eight community representative positions;[37] approximately 26,000 registered to vote (7,000 were registered by Head Start mothers), and the total number of votes cast was 9,124. The tripling of the number of votes was a source of satisfaction to the staff members who worked on the election and to the members of the board's election committee. In contrast with the first election, when the turnout was the subject of much public controversy and ridicule, almost

TABLE 1

Results of the First Poverty Election, 1966

District	Winner	Votes received by the winner	Total votes cast	Number of eligible voters
I	Albert Romo	54	178	65,417
II	Juan Gonzalez	96	434	49,924
III	Nancy Murphy	119	172	124,801
IV	Theresa Barajas	87	138	54,919
V	Ursula Gutierrez	274	775	47,829
VI	Samuel Anderson	125	714	47,829
VII	Evelyne Copeland	82	248	62,475

no public attention was given to the increased turnout of the second election. And no one calculated that in spite of the increased turnout the percentage was still only about 2 percent.

The results of the second election are shown in table 2. Minor changes in election district boundaries make comparison of turnouts misleading, but what is noticeable is that once again the poverty areas had large turnouts (the only area with a higher turnout was VIII and this voting took place almost completely at a Veterans Administration hospital where one of the candidates was in residence). The districts that cover the largest geographical area and include poverty people who are widely dispersed did not exhibit as much voter interest.

Whether the low turnout deserves criticism is debatable. On the one hand, even though low income people are least likely to vote in traditional elections, a much larger percentage appears to vote in traditional national elections than in the poverty elections.[38] On the other hand, many traditional local elections in which there are no issues, party affiliations, or preexisting cleavages of interest have a very low turnout even in middle class districts.[39] And those who defend the poverty election turnout point out that poverty elections are not traditional and encounter so many problems, including administrative difficulties, that any turnout is impressive.

But debate over the turnout should not obscure the fact that even for those who voted the election did not represent a deliberation process of any consequence. "In the process of selecting candidates there is little chance to find contestants with charisma, or even with some identification to more than next-door neighbors. The candidates by and large have no reputation for concern with the problems the election purports to address. They have no public or political record

TABLE 2

Results of the Second Poverty Election, 1968

District	Winner	Votes received by the winner	Total votes cast[a]
I	Juanita Morales	449	818
II	Rudy Aquilar	415	607
III	Dolores Shaw	322	652
IV	Jesus Flores	417	843
V	Ursula Gutierrez	534	1,359
VI	Sarah Tarver	359	1,895
VII	Eve Berry	524	1,175
VIII	Joseph Alexander	1,348	1,539

[a] No figures are available on the number of eligible voters in the revised election districts.

of accomplishment or belief. They have no established, credible, visible organization behind their candidacy."[40] Candidates in Los Angeles poverty elections seemed to gain votes mainly by what Lee has termed the politics of acquaintance.[41] Votes were based primarily on personal acquaintance with the candidate or with someone who knew him. In the second election there was evidence that the politics of what Lee called group mobilization was increasing, but the relationship of candidates to supporting organizations was obscure.[42]

The conclusion from a consideration of the Los Angeles poverty elections is that whether intentionally or unintentionally, the elections so far have been merely symbolic.[43] The system of direct general election in which all poor people were eligible to vote whether they lived in poverty pockets or not made it difficult for the representatives to develop a power base. And the elected representatives were not chosen by and thus could not speak for any organized segment of the poverty community, as is shown by the low turnout and the politics of acquaintance involved.[44] This fact does not necessarily indicate that the elections ought to be abolished, but it does suggest that at the present time they fall far short of the criteria of an election that contributes to effective representation.[45] The potential for manipulating these elections seems very high. Any organized groups, either militant or reactionary, willing to spend money to get certain individuals elected would have an easy task.

II: THE FINDINGS
★ ★ ★ ★ ★ ★ ★ ★ ★

3. The Board Members

The preceding section discussed the setting against which the results of this study should be viewed, describing the research methods used and the background of the national and Los Angeles war on poverty program. We now turn our attention to a consideration of the findings of this interview and observation study of the functioning of the EYOA board.

First, we analyze the characteristics of the board members, both the community representatives and the other participants; we want to know why they are on the board and who they are. For the purposes of analysis board members are classified as either agency or community representatives. While the distinction between the community representatives and the other board members is made by all board members, it is difficult to find a term to describe the board members who are not community representatives. The community representatives usually refer to the other members as professionals, a term they use to connote a college education and a white shirt and tie. But these characteristics do not strictly differentiate the community representatives from the others (the male community representatives wear white shirts and ties to board meetings; one has a college degree, while four of the agency board members do not). And the term professional would not describe all the other board members to their own satisfaction (they point out there are lay people and politicians in the group). Consequently the classification "agency representative" is used here to refer to the board members who are not community representatives, since the entity they represent is the only variable (besides income) which differentiates all of them from all the community representatives.

Agency representatives are further classified as either public or private agency people. The public ones represent the Los Angeles city and county governments and the city and county schools. The private ones represent the following organizations: the League of California Cities, the Los Angeles County Federation of Coordinating Councils, United Way, the Welfare Planning Council, and the AFL-CIO. These are mainly established civic and charitable groups with close links to the governmental agencies; no Negro or Mexican-American organizations are included. Community representatives are further divided into the first or second group of elected representatives. The first group was chosen in the March 1966 election and the second in the March 1968 election.

RECRUITMENT

A noticeable feature of the recruitment of board members is their low rate of turnover.[1] Ten of the twenty-four voting members were on the board for the full two years and ten months between the formation of the board in September 1965 and its restructuring in July 1968. These ten were all agency representatives, consequently almost two-thirds of the agency participants were full term members. And a total of twenty-one board members including seven of the community representatives served for at least two years. The low rate of turnover stands in marked contrast with the high rate of turnover of the staff of EYOA and the Office of Economic Opportunity.[2] The length of experience of the community representatives also contrasts with the Brandeis findings that community representatives had been on CAA boards for much shorter times than the agency representatives.[3]

The Joint Powers Agreement sets up the formal requirements for selecting the public agency representatives, but the various public agencies followed different strategies in choosing their representatives.[4] The city has always picked a Negro and a Mexican-American, and at least two of the city representatives have been from the Mayor's staff.[5] The county has not picked members of minority groups. Originally two of its representatives were from top positions in line departments, probation and public assistance[6] and one was a county supervisor. But owing to an apparent change in county strategy, these three representatives resigned within a month of one another and were replaced by subordinate staff members representing the chief administrative officer or staff departments.[7] The city schools like the city have consistently included a Negro and a Mexican-American in their delegation to the board. The third city schools representative was the member of the superintendent's staff responsible for programs for the disadvantaged. The county schools did not pick representatives from minority groups but chose two with major responsibilities for programs for the poor and one from its board of education.[8] None of the private agencies has picked members of minority groups. Two of them have chosen people by position.[9] Two others have designated members who have been active on their boards and showed a willingness to serve on EYOA.[10]

When agency representatives were asked why they were chosen by their agencies, two of them said it was because of their jobs in the agencies. Seven of these had worked closely with the Youth Opportunities Board as board members or liaison staff for their agencies. All their jobs were related to programs for the disadvantaged. The career patterns of these ten agency representatives seem to reflect differences in motivation. Five apparently were chosen for their positions within the agencies partly because of their previous interest in working in the poverty community. The educators had either been administrators working in disadvantaged areas or interested in problem students; the city and county representatives also had had contact with the problems of poverty. The careers of the other five agency representatives do not suggest prior interest, and they were picked for their agency jobs for other reasons. Another way of differentiating the motivations of agency representatives chosen for EYOA because of their jobs would be in terms of their career aspirations.[11] Approximately half of the ten agency representatives chosen for EYOA by position indicated that their performance on the board could enhance their future careers. The others indicated that EYOA was quite distinct from their other job responsibilities and would not help them advance in their jobs.

The agency representatives who were not chosen because of their jobs said they were chosen either because of their ethnic ties or because they were interested enough to contribute the time. The careers of all these agency representatives showed previous interest in poverty. But their future careers probably would not directly benefit because of their participation in EYOA. Regardless of whether they were picked because of their positions, community ties, or willingness to serve, a majority of the agency representatives would agree that they were picked because no one higher in their organizations wanted the job so it gravitated to their level.[12] Many of the agency representatives questioned the motivations of other agency represen-tatives;[13] they felt they were just assigned to be on the board and lacked previous interest in problems of poverty, and they suspected that other agency representatives were mainly concerned with fur-thering their own careers.

The agency representatives expressed more interest in the ques-tion of why the community representatives had decided to run for election than in why the agency representatives were on the board, since they correctly perceived that a majority of agency representa-tives were picked because of their positions. The agency representa-tives agreed that the community representatives ran primarily because they sincerely wanted to help solve the problems of poverty by telling the "establishment" what the real situation was. The stress was upon their commitment, since poverty is an important issue for them even if it is not important to some of the agency representatives. The com-munity representatives's motives were described as not being the tra-ditional political motives of power. The agency people said that the community representatives were not demagogues, which could have been the case if affluent people had been allowed to run for the com-munity representative positions. They were also described as not, for the most part, the slogan-shouting, demonstration-leading types out to create conflict. Some of the agency representatives did cite cases of individual community representatives they thought were motivated by the prestige of being on such a board, or by the chance to defend a certain organization or area, but these were seen as exceptions. This expressed trust of the motives of community representatives among the agency representatives contrasts with their attitude toward one another and the community representatives' attitudes toward one another which are described later.

There are some noticeable differences in how the first and sec-ond groups of community representatives say they decided to run.[14] Five of the original representatives indicated they took the initiative in inquiring about running (see table 3). Four of these said they heard announcements on the radio, or TV, or saw them in the news-paper and then called the agency that was advertising to find out the details; one of them saw announcements of the election at a Neighborhood Adult Participation Project office two doors away from his home. Some of his friends worked there and in response to his questions about running, they said, "go ahead if you think you can do it but don't expect any help." On the other hand, three of the original representatives said people asked them to run. One of these said a

TABLE 3

How Community Representatives Decided to Run

Reason	Old	New
Took the initiative	5	3
Were asked to run	3	4

neighbor asked him to run; he discovered later that the neighbor was a member of a community organization. Another said people in his community spoke to him about it but he did not link these people with any organization. A third explained that he was encouraged to run by a leader of a community organization. Only two of the eight original community representatives indicated that they were involved in organizations related to the war on poverty before they ran for election.

Turning to the second set of community representatives, only three indicated that they took the initiative in inquiring about running, and none of these did so in response to the mass media. They were at meetings of organizations related to the poverty program and heard staff members talk about the election and need for candidates. The other four new representatives said that people asked them if they would be interested in running. In three cases these were staff members of delegate agencies in which the representatives participated.

Responses of the new representatives revealed the increased importance of poverty program staffs in recruitment (all seven new community representatives referred to staff people urging candidates to run) and the increased involvement of the new representatives in organizations related to the war on poverty (six of the new were involved and only two of the former ones were). These recruitment patterns suggested that the poverty program is increasingly creating its own clientele and independent sources of community involvement are not evident.[15] A comparison of the responses of the two groups of community representatives also shows the growing importance of EYOA efforts to recruit candidates. Three community representatives specifically mention members of the EYOA staff coming to their organization to urge candidates to run. EYOA's ability to influence the election is obvious.[16] The candidates' comments on why they decided to run reinforce the general comments made in the preceding chapter about the election. The community representatives lacked an independent power base. When representatives were encouraged to run by members of organizations, the organizations were delegate agencies of EYOA.

The six new community representatives who participated in poverty programs were asked how they got involved in these programs. Three of them said that someone had come to ask them personally to go to a poverty meeting. This personal contact came from a neighbor already involved, or from paid workers recruiting by going door-to-door. The community representatives explained why they responded to the initial personal contact in vivid terms that illustrate how organizational recruitment occurs when an individual's personal needs are met. One said: "Once you go and see the people there, you get talking and you forget your troubles at home and you get involved in the community. You don't have any troubles of your own and you have the community's troubles to think about afterwards. And you know that takes that drag out of life. . . . I mean you have to do something to live for. Cause you just can't go on living for someone else and not your own. Gives you satisfaction. You know you are living and doing something." Another one said: "I was separated and I was sitting here by myself. . . . I figured it [the poverty organization] would keep me busy and I won't have so much time to think. Then I got interested. It was doing me good and it was something when you did a job you could look back and see a change, and I figured it would be better for my kids if I helped it. Maybe if I start laying the groundwork now they will have a better city to live in when they are teenagers."

For both of these representatives participation in organizations was a relatively new experience. One explained that he had been interested in getting involved but never had been because of family obligations, but when the personal contact was made he decided the time had come. The other representative explained that he had been working so had never been involved in organizations to any extent, but even when he was not working, he was hesitant to get involved. He explained: "I felt like, well, what have I got to offer really? I always thought a chairman of something was really a bigwig, someone powerful!" Thus three of the community representatives needed the stimulus of personal invitation to overcome their hesitations about organizational involvement.

The other three community representatives explained that they got involved in poverty organizations by initiating inquiries themselves. Two went to poverty organizations because they were not satisfied with their jobs at the time, and one went to the poverty organization headquarters that was next door to where he was living because he wanted to be part of "this new breed coming in to help our people."[17]

The social science interest in why poor people get involved in organizations reveals the biases of researchers. The insulting implication is that poor people are different from other people, that they join or fail to join for different reasons. The above recruitment description suggests that poor people join organizations for the same types of reasons that people who are not poor join—that is, they are exposed to the opportunity,[18] it fulfills a need, and other constraints do not prohibit the involvement. The difference is not in the reasons for joining but in the circumstances in which most poor people live. These circumstances are what must be looked at to explain why low income correlates with low organizational membership.

Recruitment of community representatives involves not only deciding to run but also campaigning and winning the election. Only two of the original community representatives mentioned having received help from any organizations, and these were not poverty groups.[19] The new community representatives mentioned getting help from a variety of poverty organizations, especially Head Start. They reported that members of these organizations helped on their own time and supplied lists of names that were used for mailings and door-to-door contacts to register voters. But in spite of these differences between the original and the new representatives, both groups mentioned the same types of campaign techniques: they used posters, throwaways, mailings, door-to-door contact, car caravans, and attended meetings of poverty and community organizations as well as special election meetings. The financial outlays were small, ranging from $10 to $100, with no reimbursement for expenses from EYOA; materials were usually donated by friends or local businesses.[20] The time investments varied; some spent most of their time campaigning in the month preceding the election and enlisted the help of family and friends; others spent little time on the campaign. But in general the campaigns were very haphazard. Even those who were assisted by poverty organization personnel did not have a strategy. The candidates tried to get the people they knew and the people in their own poverty organizations to vote for them. The campaigns fit Lee's descriptions of the politics of acquaintance and group mobilization.[21]

The representatives' vague responses about the other candidates running in their districts and why they had won also support this description of the election. The representatives had almost no knowledge of the other candidates or of who was supporting them. Some indicated they had met some of the other candidates at meetings, but several representatives had missed those meetings. The community representatives did not know who their strongest opponents were until they saw the vote results. Similarly, the representatives could not explain who their own supporters were or why they had won. It is not unusual for voters to be vague about who candidates are and who is supporting the different candidates, but in the poverty election the lack of information among the voters is paralleled by that among the candidates. The election is at the opposite end of the spectrum from an organized contest in which forces contend against other forces for the support of voters. In the poverty election lone individuals use whatever contacts they have to get people to vote. The question is not who an individual will vote for, but which individuals will vote. The aim is not to convince voters that candidate X is the best, but merely to get certain people to vote.

Related to the question of why representatives decided to run and how they campaigned is the question of the original community representatives' decision about whether to run for reelection. Three of the original representatives did run for reelection and five did not. Four of those who did not run said they were no longer eligible to run.[22] One said that he did not run because he knew he did not have a chance of winning. Of the three who did run for reelection, two said they had seriously considered not running but finally decided to run. One of these said he made the decision so people would not be able to say he had given up. The other said he chose to run because he felt the other candidates were tied to specific organizations that had wanted to get rid of him.

Only one incumbent was reelected. Is there a trend in the poverty community to vote against incumbents because they had "sold out?"[23] This would contrast with the pattern shown in the voting studies where incumbency appears to be a valuable asset in elections.[24] The negative value of incumbency in poverty elections might also be supported by evidence that the incumbent who won was viewed by respondents as the most militant of the three running for reelection. The hypothesis is not supported, however, even by the three cases at hand, because there is no evidence that the two incumbents who lost did so as a result of a negative vote, that is, by people voting for other candidates because they did not want the incumbents. In fact, one of the incumbents in losing got twice as many votes as he got the first time in winning, and he lost by only fifty votes.[25] It is quite possible that those who voted for the winner did not know anything at all about the incumbent, but voted instead because they knew the other candidate and liked him. The other losing incumbent said that he knew in advance he would lose because his personal situation made campaigning impossible, but he got more votes than he expected.

SOCIOECONOMIC CHARACTERISTICS

A description of the socioeconomic characteristics of the EYOA board members is handicapped by the absence of relevant standards of comparison. Literature on the characteristics of legislators and administrators[26] stresses the underrepresentation of the lower classes. Since the community action agency boards are specifically designed to include one-third low economic groups, they are naturally more representative than the groups traditionally studied. A more relevant standard of comparison for the EYOA board would be the other CAA boards, but only fragmentary data exist.[27] Consequently, the main emphasis here is on providing a composite picture of EYOA board members, comparing the agency representatives both public and private with the community representatives, and the old community representatives with the new ones. It is hoped this information will be useful for later comparative studies of the relationship between the composition and functioning of boards.

Age, Sex, Race, and Religion

As shown in table 4, the average age of the different groups of representatives varies.[28] The private agency representatives have the oldest average age, 56, and the narrowest spread of ages, all of them being in their fifties or sixties. The public agency representatives and the old community representatives have similar average ages, the middle forties. The new community representatives have the youngest average age, in the early forties. But notice that both the old and

TABLE 4

Age of the Board Members

	Community representatives		Agency representatives	
Age	Old	New	Public	Private
20–29	0	1	0	0
30–39	3	3	2	0
40–49	2	3	6	0
50–59	1	1	3	3
60–69	2	0	0	2
Average age	47	41	46	56

the new community representatives have wider spans of ages than the agency representatives. Three of the original community representatives were in their thirties and the new group of community representatives has one in the twenties and three in the thirties. Thus community representatives include the younger age groups not present in the other groups.[29]

The community representatives also include a higher proportion of women than the representatives from the agencies. Both the original and new community representatives included five women. Thus five out of the eight community representatives are women, whereas only two out of the other seventeen board members are women.[30] While community representatives were not included on community action boards explicitly to give representation to youth or women, they were included explicitly to give representation to minority ethnic groups which make up large shares of the poverty population. Accordingly, the fact that seven out of eight of the original community representatives in Los Angeles were Negro or Mexican-American and that only four out of the other seventeen board members were from these minority groups is not unexpected.[31] Although the original community group included three Negroes and four Mexican-Americans, the new group has only two Negroes and four Mexican-Americans.[32] Fears voiced before the first election that the districts would make it hard for Mexican-Americans to get elected have proved groundless. When the variable of sex is added to the racial breakdown (table 5) one sees that in both groups there have been two male and two female Mexican-Americans, but that in the second group there are no Negro males from the poverty community. Data on the religious backgrounds of the board members do not

TABLE 5

Ethnic Identity and Sex of the Community Representatives

Ethnic identity and sex	Old	New
Negro males	1	0
Negro females	2	2
Mexican-American males	2	2
Mexican-American females	2	2
Other males	0	1
Other females	1	1

Note: Change in ethnic identity and sex in the new group: loss of 1 Negro male, addition of 1 Caucasian male.

reveal much more than could be surmised from the ethnic backgrounds on the board. The Mexican-Americans on the board are Catholics, the Negroes are Protestants, and there are three Jews.[33]

Length of Residence in Los Angeles and Previous Residences

On the average, the community representatives have been living in Los Angeles for a shorter time than either the public or private agency representatives (see table 6). In the case of the new commu-

TABLE 6

Length of Residence in Los Angeles of the Board Members

Residence	Community representatives		Agency representatives	
	Old	New	Public	Private
Average age of arrival in Los Angeles	24	16	17	15
Average years of residence[a]	18	26	30	40

[a]Two new community representatives and one agency representative left Los Angeles for intermittent periods, but this was not included in the calculation.

nity representatives this merely indicates that they are younger than the public or private agency representatives since all three groups had a similar average age of arrival in Los Angeles. But the original community representatives not only were here a shorter length of time than the others but came at an older average age.[34] The newly elected community representatives have lived in Los Angeles longer than the original community representatives even though the new ones are younger. The native poor rather than the recent immigrant have gained seats on the board.

As one would expect, almost all the community representatives who grew up outside Los Angeles came from the South and Southwest. In contrast, all except one of the agency representatives who did not grow up in Los Angeles came from the Middle West or the West. There were no noticeable differences in the proportions of the groups coming from large cities. Both groups had members from large cities such as Dallas and Minneapolis as well as from small rural towns such as Sterling, Colorado. Some community and some agency representatives said they grew up on farms.

Social Class

The data relevant to the class origins of the board members shown in table 7 reveal some interesting patterns. If the occupations

TABLE 7

Occupations of the Board Members' Fathers

	Community representatives		Agency representatives	
Occupational category[a]	*Old*	*New*	*Public*	*Private*
Professionals	1	1	1	1
Proprietors and officials	1	2	3	4
Farmers	0	0	4	0
Low-salaried workers	0	0	1	0
Industrial wage earners, farm laborers, and servants	6	5	2	0

[a]Occupational categories follow Matthews, *U.S. Senators*, pp. 17–21.

of the members' fathers are used as indicators of class origins,[35] only three of the sixteen agency representatives' fathers were in the low-salaried or wage-earner categories. In contrast, six out of eight of the original community representatives had fathers in these groups and five out of eight of the new community representatives did.[36] The absence of professional occupations among the fathers of agency representatives is also noticeable. Not one agency representative

mentioned having a father who was a teacher or a lawyer. Only one
mentioned having a father who was a minister, and only one mentioned having a parent who was a doctor. There was instead a preponderance of merchants, bankers, real estate men, and farmers.

The data on educational level of the members' parents shown in
table 8 support the patterns of parents' occupations. While individual
community representatives had parents with more education than

TABLE 8

Education of the Board Members' Parents

	Community representatives		Agency representatives	
Education[a]	Old	New	Public	Private
Completed four years of college	0	0	3	2
Completed twelfth grade	1	1	5	1
Some high school	1	1	0	0
Completed eighth grade or less	6	6	3	2

[a]Parents are categorized according to the highest level reached by either one
of them.

certain agency representatives, the education of the parents of most
agency representatives was markedly higher than that of the parents
of the community representatives. Five agency representatives had at
least one parent with a college degree, but no community representatives did. And six agency representatives had at least one parent who
had completed the twelfth grade, but only one original and one new
community representative did. Only five agency representatives said
their parents had an eighth-grade education or less, but six community representatives in both the first and the second groups were in
this category.[37] Several community representatives with parents from
Mexico and from the South mentioned that at least one of their parents could not write.

Using the criteria of occupation and education, the agency
representatives have shown marked upward mobility when compared
with their parents. Whereas eleven of their fathers were proprietors
and two were professionals, now five of the agency representatives
are proprietors (several with incomes above $30,000) and eleven
are classified as professionals (see table 9).[38] The latter group includes five educators, one minister, and five governmental officials
(these five include two with backgrounds in management, and one

each in engineering, journalism, and social work).[39] All except four of the agency representatives have at least a college degree, two have

TABLE 9

Occupations of the Board Members

Occupational category[a]	Community representatives		Agency representatives	
	Old	New	Public	Private
Professional	0	0	11	0
Proprietors and officials	0	1	0	5
Farmers	0	0	0	0
Low-salaried workers	2	2	0	0
Industrial wage earners, farm laborers, and servants	6	5	0	0

[a]See Matthews, U.S. Senators, pp. 17–21, for explanation of the occupational categories.

doctorates, and five have other graduate degrees. The contrast between their high level of education and their parents' educations can be seen by comparing the data in table 10 with table 8.

TABLE 10

Education of the Board Members

Education	Community representatives		Agency representatives	
	Old	New	Public	Private
Graduate degree	0	. .	7	0
Completed four-year college	0	1	3	2
Some college	7	2	0	2
Completed twelfth grade	0	3	1	0
Some high school	0	2	0	1
Completed eighth grade	1	0	0	0

The mobility of the community representatives when compared with their families is not so clear. As shown in table 9, all except one of the community representatives would still fall in the low-salaried or wage-earner classes.[40] Some of these community representatives feel they are better off than their families, but since the general pattern of the population has been one of a rising standard of living this feeling does not in itself indicate intergenerational upward mobility. The level of education among the community representatives is noticeably higher than their parents', however, even though their occupational classes are not (compare table 10 with table 8). It may seem extraordinary, but seven of the original community representatives had had some schooling beyond the twelfth grade and only one had not finished high school.[41] Most of the new community representatives have not had as much education as the original community representatives. One does have a college degree, but only two others have done work beyond the twelfth grade. Three others had stopped after finishing high school, and one stopped after finishing the eleventh grade, and one after the tenth grade. Yet even though all the community representatives had more education than their parents, just as the agency representatives had, the community representatives were not able to improve their occupational position significantly. They seem merely to have kept up with the national rise in educational level.[42]

The contrast between the community and agency representatives is further confirmed by the respondents' own subjective class identification. Most of the agency representatives described themselves as either middle class or upper middle class,[43] whereas almost all the community representatives described themselves as working class or lower class.[44]

Type of Education and Career

Information on the education and occupational history of board members lends itself to analysis that goes beyond crude designations of differences in class and mobility. It allows one to make qualitative distinctions among the types of educations and careers pursued by the board members. The agency representatives characteristically went to state universities for their Bachelor's degrees and majored in English (6), economics (2), business administration, history, and psychology. The largest number went to the University of California, Los Angeles, for undergraduate work (6). Five respondents indicated they had attended private colleges, including Pomona, Oberlin and Kenyon, Occidental, Duke, and DePauw University. The university that most respondents attended for graduate degrees was the University of Southern California, four respondents completing graduate education degrees there. In contrast, if the community representatives did attend college at all, they went to junior colleges or state colleges, not state universities.[45]

The career patterns of the two groups contrast markedly. The

agency representatives exhibit stability in the organizations they
work for, and the type of jobs performed. Seven have continued in
the same field throughout their entire working lives and four of these
have always worked for the same organization. The other agency
representatives have typically stayed in similar kinds of work and
have worked for only two different organizations.[46] When the community representatives were asked to describe their jobs, they reeled
off a staggering list of diverse hourly jobs and employing organizations. For example, a community representative in his thirties gave
the following for a start: sewing machine operator, clerk, laundry
marker, stock transfer clerk for the Bank of America, bookkeeper for
the Department of Motor Vehicles, nurse's aide. Another young
representative listed the following jobs: quarantine inspector, surgi-
cal technician, electronics assembler, garment industry worker, private nurse, supermarket security officer, and convalescent home aide.
The community representatives' careers illustrate the meaning of
unstable employment and low paid, unsatisfying work. Several mentioned repeated periods of unemployment and of being on welfare.
The lack of educational credentials and the pressing need for money
mean that the community representatives repeatedly have to take
whatever hourly work they can find and the result is the erratic pattern that they exhibit.

The contrasts are illuminated further by the aspirations of the
two groups. The overwhelming majority of agency representatives
said, when asked what their career hopes were for the future, that they
hoped to be in the same type of job and same organization, but on
a higher level. Virtually all the agency representatives said it is quite
likely they would remain in the Los Angeles area.[47] One respondent
explained that the thought of moving out of his organization has occurred to him and that a different type of person with a less conservative life style might have been "long gone" because many of those
involved in the early poverty activities were in positions that could
have been springboards "to something or other."

The tone of almost all the responses from community representatives was that they were still hoping to improve the situation either
for themselves or for their children. They wanted to change their
current jobs and get into a line of work that would allow them to develop meaningful careers. Like the agency representatives, however,
they were almost unanimous in indicating that it was likely they

would stay in Los Angeles. Three of the original community representatives talked about completing college, and two mentioned that although they were too old, their children were going to get educations and improve their conditions. Five expressed an interest in jobs with poverty organizations, one in teaching, and one in being a parole officer.[48] The new community representatives' comments were very similar.

So the EYOA board is made up of one group with high education and stable careers and one group with lower education and extremely unstable jobs, but with aspirations for more stability. Yet the groups share a similar attachment to the Los Angeles area.

Family Stability

Family stability also appears to be a significant differentiator between the agency representatives and the community representatives.[49] None of the agency representatives indicated that they were divorced or separated. But three of the new and four of the original community representatives are divorced or separated and half of these have been divorced or separated more than once.[50] To this instability plus the instability of low income must be added the fact that while almost all agency representatives own their homes, less than half the community representatives do.[51] Further indication of the stresses on the families is that while only three agency representatives have more than two children, six of the original community representatives do. An interesting change is that only three of the new community representatives have more than two children.

Organizational and Political Participation

One characteristic of the board members which is particularly important to this study is their participation in both politics and organizations. As one would expect, the agency representatives are characterized by involvement in many organizations, as illustrated in table 11. Ten out of sixteen agency representatives listed membership in three or more organizations. The most frequently mentioned types of groups were service organizations such as Rotary and Kiwanis, community coordinating councils, and professional organizations. The agency representatives not only belonged to large numbers of organizations but also were officeholders in well over 75 percent of the organizations they listed.

The organizational participation of the private agency representatives is greater than the public agency representatives; private representatives typically belong to four or more organizations, with the number going higher than ten in two cases. This indicates that their own jobs either involve organizational membership or allow

TABLE 11

Organizational Participation of the Board Members

	Community representatives[a]		Agency representatives	
Participation	Old	New	Public	Private
Belong to four or more organizations	0	1	2	3
Belong to three organizations	0	3	4	1
Belong to two organizations	5	2	3	1
Belong to one organization	1	2	1	0
Belong to none	2	0	1	0

[a]Organizational membership before joining the board

them time for hyperactivity.[52] The public agency representatives, on the other hand typically belong to three organizations. Apparently their jobs take up a major portion of their time and while the jobs may involve much contact with community organizations, they do not entail membership in those organizations.[53]

When the organizational activity of the agency representatives is compared with the respondents' recollections of their parents' organizational activity, one finds indications of increased activity.[54] Table 12 shows that seven of the agency representatives are more active in community affairs than their parents were and three of these show a large increase in activity—that is, their parents were hardly active but they themselves belong to four or more community service organizations.[55]

Turning to the community representatives, both the original and the new community representatives belonged to fewer organizations when they joined the board than did the agency representatives (table 11), and most of the community representatives had not held offices in their organizations. As indicated in the discussion about the recruitment of community representatives, the new representatives belonged to more organizations when they were elected than did the original representatives.[56] The most frequently mentioned types of groups were churches and religious organizations for the first set of representatives and war-on-poverty related organizations for the second set. While it is not surprising to find that community representatives were less involved in organizations than agency representatives,

TABLE 12

Comparison of Community Activity of Board Members and Their Parents

Degree of activity	Community representatives		Agency representatives	
	Old	New	Public	Private
More active than parents	3	5	5	2
Similar activity	4	2	6	3
Less active than parents	1	1	0	0

the community representatives were more active prior to joining the board than the literature on low-income organizational participation would suggest.[57] This level of involvement may be partly an artifact of the war on poverty, since five of the new community representatives indicated that before the war on poverty they did not belong to any organization.

The results of a comparison of the community representatives and their parents in terms of organizational activity are mixed. At the time of their election, four of the community representatives would fall in the same category as their parents; three were already more active than their parents.[58] At the time the new community representatives were elected, five were more active than their parents were, two were about the same, and one was less active. Thus the new community representatives show a slight tendency to have been more active when compared with their parents than the old community representatives were, as shown in table 12.

There were some marked differences in the reported interest of parents in politics between the original community representatives and the new ones. Six of the original community representatives said their parents were hardly interested in politics at all, but only three of the new community representatives said this. But the two groups of community representatives expressed similar high interest in politics by the time they were elected to the board. They said they followed politics and voted in elections. Only one community representative admitted to never having voted prior to his vote in the 1968 local elections. While the new community representatives seemed more active in community organizations than the original ones, and as interested in politics, none of them indicated they had worked on campaigns, although three of the original community representatives said they had worked on campaigns.

The organizational and political participation of the community representatives reveals the way in which the representatives recruited for the EOYA board reflect the election system. They are not loners; they have belonged to organizations. But they have generally not been leaders or spokesmen in their organizations and have not been well known in their communities. Membership on the policy-making board of EYOA does involve a marked change in their level of participation. Furthermore, their organizational memberships do not provide them with an independent, organized constituency; as representatives they do not have clear ties with community organizations. So the election system that makes it difficult for representatives to have a power base also recruits community people with less experience in organizations and weaker ties with their constituencies than the agency representatives.

TYPOLOGY OF THE MEMBERS

A review of the characteristics of the board members suggests that the two groups of representatives, agency and community, reflect the differences in their recruitment. As a group the agency people are differentiated from the community representatives along many dimensions. The agency representatives are older, and longer residents of Los Angeles; they include more males, Caucasians, and Westerners; they have more schooling, higher occupational status, more stable careers and families, and greater participation in organizations and politics. Conversely, the community representatives are younger, newer residents of Los Angeles; they include more women, minority members, and Southerners; and they have less schooling, lower occupational status, less stable careers and families, and less participation in organizations and politics. Both groups showed upward mobility from their parents' occupations, education, and participation. But in general the parents of the community representatives were more disadvantaged than the agency representatives' parents, and the community representatives had not improved their positions relative to their parents as much as the agency representatives had. These differences are consistent with social science generalizations about poverty and the middle class; their confirmation by the data serves to underscore the gap between the two main groups on the board.

TABLE 13

Typology of Board Members

Private agency representatives	Community representatives
4 lay people	1 stable poor
1 labor representative	3 strained
Public agency representatives	5 copers
5 educators	5 unstable poor
3 bureaucrats[a]	1 (other)
3 politicians[b]	
1 lay person	

[a]At least one of the bureaucrats thinks like a politician; Krosney uses the term "policrat" to describe this type. *Beyond Welfare: Poverty in the Supercity.*
[b]One of the politicians might be classified as a bureaucrat.

The data on board members also enables us to make differentiations within the two primary groups, as shown in table 13. The private agency representatives, reflecting the civic and welfare organizations they come from, are predominantly lay people and are older, wealthier, and more active in community organizations than the public agency representatives. The public agency representatives are predominantly educators, and most have careers closely linked with the agencies that send them to EYOA. Some of them had not shown previous interest in poverty, but were given the board assignment because of positions they held within their agencies. Their future jobs may be affected by their performance on the board.

The public agency representatives can be divided rather arbitrarily into four types—educators, bureaucrats, politicians, and laymen. Little comparative information exists on the outlooks of different occupational groups[59] but it seems likely that the different training, organizational and occupational identification, and situational constraints of the various types of board members mean they have characteristic viewpoints. Banfield finds this true for politicians and bureaucrats and the argument can be extended to the other groups.[60] Using existing typologies of politicians, two of the politicians on EYOA would fall into the category of professional politician; but one's career would follow the traditional pattern of working within the party, and the other's would be linked specifically with a particular elected official.[61] Using Reissman's typology of bureaucrats, two of the board members would be job bureaucrats, looking for recognition within the bureaucracy itself and stressing efficiency. One would be a specialist, identifying with the bureaucracy and a professional group.[62]

All the public agency representatives hold boundary positions in their organizations.[63] Consequently they are subject to special stresses; they are blamed by outsiders for shortcomings in their own organizations which they cannot control, and they come into conflict with individuals within their basically conservative, rules-oriented organization who have a vested interest in the status quo. Organizations choose people of high self-confidence, mobility, aspirations, and job involvement for these boundary jobs.[64] These characteristics would generally apply to the agency representatives on the EYOA board; they appear more sympathetic to the poverty program and social change than the average member of their agencies. Accordingly, the agency representatives may be thought of not as typical agency members, but rather as deviant educators, bureaucrats, and politicians.

Data on board members also allow us to make differentiations within the group of community representatives. Using Reissman's typology of working class and lower class, almost all the community representatives would be considered lower class because they are marked by instability in their jobs, families, and neighborhoods.[65] A more useful typology for distinguishing among the community representatives is Miller's, which combines two variables, economic and familial stability, to arrive at a fourfold classification. The stable poor are those with high stability on both indicators; the strained are those with economic security but familial insecurity; the copers are characterized by economic insecurity but familial security; and the unstable poor are characterized by instability on both indicators.[66] Miller discusses the shortcomings of the indicators he uses and these become painfully apparent when attempts are made to place the community representatives in these categories. Nevertheless it is possible to make impressionistic classifications. When both the original and new community representatives are classified (see table 12) the largest number fall in the categories of unstable poor and copers (five in each); three could be considered strained, and only one seems to clearly fit the stable poor category.[67]

Just as the agency representatives can be seen as atypical, so can the community representatives. The agency representatives described the community representatives as being pretty close to middle class. They said that the community people share middle-class values; do not make conflict for conflict's sake; and do not reflect the "nitty gritty" of extreme poverty. And it is true that most of the community representatives did not identify themselves as lower class, but as working class. Further, their level of participation in organizations and politics and their aspirations could be indicators that they are deviant poor people. If different criteria are used, however the community representatives would seem to be in the mainstream of poverty. Economically they fall in the lowest income group.[68] Many have been on welfare and unemployed for long periods of time. The results are similar if the criteria is education or occupational and family instability. Accordingly, all comments about whether or not community representatives are deviant require careful specification of the standard of comparison, which in turn brings up the whole issue of what is a typical poor person. That issue cannot be discussed here; we can only call attention to the lack of knowledge about that part of the social structure. Social scientists must give more attention to the diversity that exists among the poor, just as it exists among all other strata of society.[69]

In answer, then, to the question of who the board members are, they are the types of people one might expect based on the board's structure and recruitment procedures. There is a predominance of career public servants, namely bureaucrats, educators, and professional politicians. And the private agency people are more similar socioeconomically to the public representatives than to the community representatives. The community people are differentiated from the public and private representatives in terms of age, sex, race, residence, income, education, occupation, family instability, and prior participation. Keeping in mind the characteristics of the board members, one can better understand the way the board members work together, which is the topic of the next chapter.

4. How the Board Functions

The board members described in the preceding chapter interact in carrying out EYOA business. The types of people they are, their backgrounds, jobs, and motivations all influence the operation of the board, but many other external factors are at work too. These external forces include the local, state, and national political structures. Accordingly, the EYOA board should not be looked upon merely as a small group but rather as a policy-making group constrained by numerous external forces.[1] Furthermore, it is possible to view the full EYOA board as one group and also to view the agency representatives and the poverty representatives as two small groups within the larger group. The following material encompasses both views of the board.

This chapter describes how the EYOA board functions. It reports on the members' perception of what they are representing, who they are speaking for on the board. Then it presents the members' opinions about what the important issues and factions are and compares these with observation. After considering the members' descriptions of their own roles and of the relative influence of other members, an attempt is made to draw together the data to answer the question of who has predominant influence on the board. In other words, judging from the way the board functions (as perceived by the members and by an observer), what forces appear to be most influential?[2]

The answer to this general question makes it possible to evaluate the relative influence of the community representatives on the functioning of the board. The literature on interactions involving power differentials among the participants leads one to expect that those who enter into the relationship with less power continue to have less power even though formally they may be equals. For example, Marris

and Rein found that even indigenous community organizations designed solely to develop participation by the poor were not effective
in devolving power to people in neighborhoods. They were not organized to assume such power, so control remained with the project
staff.[3] Similarly, the study of TVA found that community groups
were formally co-opted in order to gain legitimization. Formal co-
optation means sharing the burdens and responsibilities of power
rather than the power itself.[4] This chapter evaluates whether the community representatives in EYOA have been co-opted.

REPRESENTATION AS PERCEIVED BY THE MEMBERS

A major influence on the way the board works is the relationship
between members and the entities they represent. Agency representatives were asked what they were representing on the board and what
constraints this placed on their board activities. Wahlke and Eulau's
two types of representational role orientations, trustee and delegate,
are useful in describing the agency people's responses.[5] While the
term "agency representative" might suggest a pure delegate relationship, almost all the agency people were quick to deny that they voiced
the interests mainly of the agency that sent them to the board. Their
responses form a continuum ranging between delegate and trustee.

The private agency representatives made statements most similar to the trustee role.[6] They stressed their freedom to be more objective than the public agency or community representatives because
they did not have vested interests in any one agency or area.[7] One
stated that the board members should not represent anyone (when
he was asked who he felt he was representing, he did not understand
the question since he thought the concept was inappropriate to the
board). He said board members should be closely concerned with
seeing that the money is well spent and should disqualify themselves
from voting when issues came up in which their agency had an
interest.[8]

The representatives who talked most like delegates were those
from the public agencies.[9] These members acknowledged they wanted
to further the interests of the agency they represented. They insisted
they tried to have a more comprehensive picture, and on issues not
directly related to their agencies they were trustees. One explained
that his agency "is interested in the community so you can say I'm
representing the community also." Two said they had become more

concerned with the comprehensive picture, but one said that the reverse had happened to him. When he was first on the board he was concerned with the general welfare of the community, but increasingly he saw his job mainly as that of delegate, defending his agency against attacks.

On the topic of constraints, most of the private agency representatives said that they received no instructions from their agencies, and that all communications went from them toward their agencies rather than vice versa. But the public agency people mentioned many constraints. They cited pressures to support positions taken by their own staffs and staffs of poverty programs operated by their agencies. For example, if the choice had to be made between cutting these programs or cutting EYOA central staff, the agency representatives felt constrained to cut the latter. Similarly examples were given of pressures to support "our own people," and decisions to vote with those "who pay my salary." But only a few mentioned instances when their agency's interests conflicted with what they as individuals felt was in the best interests of EYOA.[10]

All the agency representatives, both public and private, agreed they did not get much direct pressure from people in the community although they did receive mailings from agencies that have programs and a few calls from people with complaints about funding or personnel matters. But a majority commented on the indirect pressure they felt not to antagonize the community. They cited a variety of positions they had taken not because they or their agencies thought they were wise, but because they wished to avoid hurting the community opinion of their agencies. One explained: "None of us can vote the way we feel—we always have to think what others will think of us, and how it will reflect on our agency." They talked of feeling inhibited about making the right decisions because of the presence of protesters and an angry emotional climate at some board meetings. They felt that the agency representatives had leaned over backward to avoid making decisions that would make their agencies unpopular in the community.[11]

The community board members viewed representation differently. The community representatives[12] were asked whom they represented, how they tried to keep in touch with their constituents, and what kinds of pressures they received from constituents. The community representatives said they were representing the impoverished people in their districts and not organizations.[13] Three said that the problems in the districts were so similar that they increasingly felt they were representing the interests of impoverished people in all areas. One community representative mentioned that he tried to consider both the impoverished community and the community as a whole, and if something seemed detrimental to the latter, he would oppose it.[14]

The most striking aspect of the community representatives' responses was the extreme distrust they voiced of the other community representatives' claims to really represent their communities.[15] Six community representatives described their own independence of organizations as unique; they said the other representatives were pushed to run by organizations who wanted members on the board and were linked with special interests. Some of the ones mentioned were: city hall, Congressman Hawkins, Community Service Organization, Head Start, Neighborhood Adult Participation Project (NAPP), Teen Post, labor, senior citizen organizations, and Parent Teacher associations. But the community representatives were not consistent in linking given interests with a certain representative; one representative would be linked with city hall by one subject and with Congressman Hawkins by another; with Head Start by one and with NAPP by another. When asked for evidence of the connections many admitted that the other community representatives denied the connections and no firm evidence existed, but they still felt the links existed. Observation of committee meetings showed that whenever one representative alluded to organizational links of another there was a flare-up of anger. When one community representative sponsored the cause of a community organization, the other community representatives insisted that he should not align himself with a group, but instead should try to make an objective judgment on the merits of the case.[16]

When asked how they kept in touch with their constituents, community representatives said that the task was impossible. They mentioned going to numerous meetings in the community and encouraging people to talk with them. Only one community representative maintained that he was in constant touch with citizens at the grass roots and had their complete confidence. A more typical statement was that they wished they had had help in communicating with their constituents because more could have been accomplished if they had known how to go about the job. Several mentioned the need for

an office and a telephone in the community and pointed out that
EYOA had denied requests for these.[17] Stress was also placed on the
need for getting out into the community more, not just at meetings
but also just talking with people and seeing how they felt. But representatives told of setting up community meetings and then being told
by EYOA that all meetings should be cleared with EYOA. Most
would agree with the statement made by one representative about
the difficulty of representing the poverty communities: "I don't think
that any one community representative really knows what the community wants. I don't think we speak for the community any more
than any elected official is speaking for the total community, you
know. It's just not true. I have tried to vote the way the community
that I know, that I see, wants." In other words, while their goal was
to represent their poverty community or the whole poverty community, they had a hard time judging what it wanted. This admittedly is
a problem for any geographical area representative, but at least
elected officials have assistance in the task.[18]

The agency representatives revealed diverse opinions about the
representational role of the community board members. Several implied that the main job of the community people was to disseminate
information to their communities about the poverty program in order
to build community support. Most indicated that this had not been
done well but admitted that some representatives had tried to get
acquainted with their communities. One agency representative explained: "Remember, we picked these people up in a hurry. We
called them community representatives but actually they have merely
been people who lived in a certain community, so they had to grow
into becoming community representatives."

Another typical comment was that at least the community representatives were a better link with the community than any of the
agency people could be. Other agency representatives suggested that
the main job of the community representatives was to speak for the
interests of the people in their districts. Only one agency representative thought it might be proper for community representatives to
advocate the interests of specific organizations in their districts.[19] Yet
the agency people who felt community representatives should speak
for their districts did not appear to have given much thought as to
how this could be done. And some were critical of the community

members for being "less representative of anything than anybody else on the board."

When one agency representative was asked why he felt this was the case, he said it was because there was no highly organized community to represent. This view again highlights the gap between the perspectives of agency and community representatives. The community representatives would say the difficulty in speaking for their districts was at least partly the fault of EYOA and the joint powers, because they denied them the assistance necessary for effective representation.

In spite of the community representatives' problems in speaking for their districts, five indicated they received a great deal of pressure from people in the community and got calls at all hours of the night demanding things. The pressures included insults and epithets such as "Uncle Tom," and charges that "you don't know our problems."[20] All the community members said the communications they did get were mainly from the staffs of delegate agencies or from community people participating in poverty programs who were angry about funding or personnel decisions directly affecting them. They also talked of the pressure exerted when large numbers of people came to board meetings to protest board actions. Some said that when an issue had that kind of support from the people, EYOA ought to go along with the people. Others said they no longer were swayed by numbers because they had found that often the protesters were not poor.

The statements by community members about representation lead to an interesting finding. Lacking clear ties with community organizations and unable to represent poverty people in vast geographical districts, the community representatives actually became spokesmen for aggrieved clients or staff members of the poverty program; these are their real constituents. This informal role of the community representatives suggests the need to rethink the whole function of community members on the board. They cannot really represent poor people in their community; instead they are serving as ombudsmen for poverty programs. Individuals with complaints about poverty programs go to the community members because they feel they will be more sympathetic than the agency representatives.

A review of all the board members' comments on representation suggests two general conclusions. First, board members have not given searching consideration to their assumptions about the proper roles of different types of board members.[21] There are staff memorandums[22] and an ad hoc committee report approved by the board, but these are very general formal statements on roles and have not promoted discussions of the underlying issues. Second, there are inconsistencies in the members' views of the proper roles of agency as opposed to community representatives. Agency representatives generally see nothing wrong in speaking for the interests of their own organizations because they see these organizational interests as similar to EYOA's and the community's. They are critical of community representatives who speak for specific organizational interests, however, and say they should speak for the general interests of their areas. The community representatives on the whole have accepted this view of their role; they do not consider it legitimate for them to represent specific organizations.[23] Yet many are not critical of the agency representatives speaking for organizational interests.

The community representatives seem to have gone even further than the agency representatives in accepting a unitary conception of the public good.[24] This view holds that there is such a thing as an objective public or community good which can be found by objective concern with the good of the whole. This position rejects the legitimacy of special interests and calls instead for concern with the broad picture. It contrasts with the pluralistic conception of the public good which holds that all perspectives are partial, and that it is proper for all the competing partial interests to be firmly advocated. This conception is closer to the agency representatives' idea of their own role as advocates of agency interests. By rejecting this view of their own role, the community representatives have helped cut themselves off from a meaningful constituency. The unitary view they accept prevents them from representing specific community organizations within their districts. As pointed out in chapter 2, the election system supported by the community representatives is a major factor in the absence of a power base for community representatives.[25] But they have made their position even weaker by accepting a view of their role on the board which ensures that they will not represent the organized interests that do exist in their communities and leaves them at the mercy of the powerful forces in Los Angeles.

The board members' views of representation described above help explain the functioning of the board. Their assumptions about

representation underlie the roles they play on the board, their evaluations of other board members, and the emphasis on avoiding controversy which is shown to be a central feature of the operation of the
EYOA board.

When the board members were asked about the key issues of
controversy, the usual response was that they could not think of any
key controversial issues. So two different questions were used: "What
were the most important decisions made by the board?" And "What
were the recurring vote splits on the board?" The important issues
mentioned can be grouped into three categories:[26] structure and jurisdiction, funding and programs, and personnel and procedural pol-
icies. One noticeable feature of the issues mentioned is that most of
them were linked with federal decisions.[27]

Analysis of the minutes and of notes taken during six months
of observation at board meetings (January to June 1968) supports
the respondents who said that controversial issues did not predom-
inate on the board. Only 28 percent of the votes taken during the
six-month period had any abstentions or nos.[28] An examination of
the minutes prior to January 1968 reveals basically similar patterns.

The votes on issues listed by respondents as key board decisions
were also remarkably noncontroversial. The most striking example
of the lack of controversy is provided by the decisions about the election of community representatives. The procedures for both the first
and second election were approved by an election committee made
up of interim representatives or community representatives[29] and then
supported by the board. The decision to divide the whole county into
election districts and have a general election as opposed to a conven-
tion type of election was unanimous.[30]

The fact of consensus contrasts with the public impression that
the Los Angeles war on poverty is torn by commotion and turmoil.
Reports in the media convey the image of constant picketing at
EYOA offices and screaming audiences at board meetings. But in
spite of occasionally turbulent onlookers, observation confirms that
many of the most important issues are settled by the board with little
or no debate and few dissenting votes. What accounts for this absence of controversy? An attempt to answer this question is made
after consideration of the factions and the interaction on the board.

FACTIONS AS PERCEIVED BY THE MEMBERS

Approximately half the agency representatives responded that there really were no blocs on the board.[31] They denied that agency people voted one way and community people another. They said a school representative and a community representative might be in agreement more often than a school representative and another agency representative. One subject pointed out that the establishment did not vote together because the agencies are all different—the people from the agencies have different ideas, belong to different parties, and have different theories about everything. But they admitted that on an issue that affects a given agency's programs the people from that agency vote as a bloc.

Those who say there is bloc voting are primarily from private agencies. They say the city protects its interests by voting together and the county protects its interests in a similar manner; they say the establishment votes one way and the poverty representatives vote another way.[32] It is interesting that the responses by private agency representatives are similar to the responses of the majority of community representatives. The private agency representatives feel, like the community representatives, that each public agency is on the board "to make sure that they get theirs so they can make mileage out of it."[33] It is interesting, too, that a majority of agency representatives distrust the motives of representatives from other agencies. They question the sincerity of the others' interest in poverty.[34] This suspiciousness is as marked among the agency representatives as among the community representatives.[35] The city and county representatives distrust each other; the politicians distrust the bureaucrats and vice versa. And there is distrust between the schools and the city and county, that is, between the educators on one hand and the politicians and bureaucrats on the other. There is trust, however, between the city educators and the county educators. And while the schools are suspicious of both the city politicians and county bureaucrats, some links exist between the city schools and the city so the city schools seem most suspicious of the county. The formal arrangements linking the county schools with the county (both the County Board of Education and the County Superintendent are appointed by the County Board of Supervisors) would suggest that the county schools would feel links with the county,[36] but there is some indication that the formal links are not matched by a feeling of mutuality among board representatives.[37]

The comments by agency representatives on how community representatives voted showed strong agreement (approximately 75 percent) that the community representatives did not vote as a bloc.[38] The responses of the community representative to a question about whether or not they voted as a bloc are generally in agreement with the agency representatives' view that they did not. The community representatives said they had tried to be unified but that the unity broke down. Their remarks also explain why agency representatives denied a bloc and yet some perceived a community voice in opposition to the establishment.

Five of the seven community representatives who expressed opinions on this issue said that the community representatives were quite divided.[39] They mentioned early meetings among the community representatives in several different election areas and the plan that these meetings would continue. But the meetings did not. They said that the only issue on which all the community representatives voted as a bloc was on the first major controversy to confront them on the board—the firing of Opal Jones, director of the Neighborhood Adult Participation Project.[40]

Although the community representatives disagreed on the reason for the division, there was consensus on the subgroupings among the community representatives. A group of four community representatives stuck together quite closely; the others did not. The four felt that the others had sold out—been won over by the establishment. The others gave different explanations of why unity had not been possible. Personality conflicts were frequently mentioned. Some resented what they saw as attempts by other community representatives to monopolize the voting decision and prevent the rest from using their own judgment of what was needed. There was mention of competition among these representatives for leadership, and distrust of the motives of other community representatives.

The two community representatives who denied division among the community representatives did agree that on specific issues there was indeed division, but they stressed a less tangible sense of unity, of unanimity. One explained that community representatives in spite of specific differences really thought alike; the problems in their districts were not as different as they might have thought at first.

The comments suggest that even though the community representatives did not vote as a unanimous bloc they shared the view that not enough of the money was getting down to the poor and the poor people's voices were not being given adequate attention. In addition, at least four community representatives felt they were a bloc. Thus there does seem to have been something of a community position opposed to an agency position, but the community representatives were not united in supporting this position.

INTERACTION AS REPORTED BY THE MEMBERS

Another method for discerning factions is to find out the patterns of informal interaction—who talks with whom outside board business meetings. Virtually all the agency representatives said relatively little interaction goes on outside the board meetings. The contacts that were mentioned seem to be of three types: (a) contacts within an agency; (b) contacts among people in different agencies in connection with the administration of programs; and (c) contacts with people in connection with issues coming before the board. There does not seem to be much planning of strategy among representatives of a given agency, except the county representatives. Contacts among agency people in different agencies parallel the links of trust mentioned above. The city and county schools work closely together on programs and consequently exchange casual opinions on board issues. The city schools call the city when school proposals are coming before the board and vice versa. The county seems to be the only agency that has set up meetings to discuss issues relevant to the board. And the county apparently feels freer to call other joint powers people to find out their thinking on issues, or to give them information on items on the agenda. The private agency people do not mention initiating many phone calls but do mention receiving some, especially from the county.

Note first that none of the agency representatives mentioned calling community representatives, although several mentioned that community representatives had called them for information. Second, the contacts that do occur among agency representatives seem very casual. For the most part, they involve phone calls and not meetings. But even more characteristic seems to be casual conversations before, during, and after board meetings or when the representatives are in contact over program administration. One representative described the interactions accurately as "brief encounters in the washroom or elevators." Third, most of the representatives felt the lack of contact was good; they equated informal contact with skulduggery, with getting together ahead of time and saying they were going to push certain items through, which would violate the Brown Act.[41]

The patterns of informal interaction among agency representatives support the description of factions given above. They support the view that representatives from the same agency have a certain degree of unity, which is most marked on issues affecting that agency. They also support the perception that the agency representatives have a viewpoint distinct from the community representatives' approach. The patterns of informal interaction also suggest one reason why half the agency representatives respond that no blocs exist. The agencies do not have cohesive positions on a wide variety of issues; the groupings are amorphous and shifting, not nearly as clearly defined as in some legislatures where the members are involved full time in efforts to promote given actions.

Few agency representatives had impressions of how much the community representatives interacted outside board meetings, but the ones who did suggested they did not think much interaction was going on anymore. The community representatives confirmed that the original plans for frequent informal meetings had not been followed. But they mentioned that contacts among four of them did keep up. And all the community representatives mentioned phone calls to other community representatives about board issues, and conversations in car pools, and over coffee before and after meetings. It was pointed out that community representatives usually came to board meetings an hour early to talk. The community representatives said that at times they did talk with agency representatives to try to get their support.

Comments by the respondents not only revealed patterns of who talked with whom, they also indicated the nature of the relationships among all board members. Their responses suggest that the twenty-five board members have surprisingly little knowledge about each other. At least five respondents said they could not remember the names of various board members. Agency representatives could not think of the names of public agency representatives and community representatives (one had to refer to a printed list of members' names). Community representatives asked the names of agency representatives but knew the names of the other community representatives. Respondents not only had trouble with names but they also indicated they did not know about the jobs various agency representatives held, their backgrounds, or attitudes. One member explained that since the board meets only twice a month he sees the members rarely, and very often different people are at different meetings.[42] The lack of knowledge indicates that most of the relationships and interactions among board members are very superficial.

OBSERVATION OF FACTIONS

An analysis of the voting divisions on very controversial issues before the board serves to confirm the picture of factions given by respondents. In the six-month period between January and June 1968 there were nine issues on which four or more negative votes were cast.[43] Four or more community representatives voted against the rest of the board on over half the issues. The community representatives voting negatively changed depending on the issue, but there does appear to be an identifiable community representative position of defending what they see to be the little man against the established agencies. Even though they are joined at various times by one or another of the agency representatives, on the issues where there is controversy the majority of community representatives are found, in six out of nine cases, on the losing side.[44]

The converse is that public agency representatives do tend to vote together and are usually joined by the private agency representatives on the winning side. Yet the factions among the public agency people indicated in the interviews also show in the voting. The county has been voting against the rest of the board and losing on almost half of the controversial issues. When the issue concerns feelings that EYOA staff wants the board to be a rubber stamp, the county finds itself allied with the community representatives against the EYOA staff.[45] When the issue concerns an EYOA threat to the control of county programs the community representatives are no longer allies, but some of the other similarly affected agencies may be.[46]

Observation of the seating and attendance patterns between January and June provide support for this description of factions. Since many of the board members indicated awareness of the significance of who they sit next to (and a desire not to sit in obvious blocs) it was not expected that seating would indicate factions. Yet three or four community representatives can be found sitting next to one another at most meetings. And county representatives sit together more often than do the representatives from the other public agencies. Attendance patterns show that each of the joint powers agencies usually has at least one of its representatives at each meeting,[47] but usually only two of their three representatives are present. The county sends all three representatives more often than the other agencies.[48] The obvious result is that public agency representatives do not have as high an attendance record as the other representatives, especially the community representatives, as shown in Appendix II. The agencies apparently are careful to have someone attend to represent their interests but do not feel the need to use all their votes on most issues. When, however, an issue of particular concern to a public agency is on the agenda, such as an agency program proposal, more of its representatives are present and vote in a bloc.

ROLES AND INFLUENCE IN THE GROUP

The respondents' comments on the roles they saw themselves filling and on the influential board members are indicative of the culture of the board, the norms or rules of the game followed by the members.[49] This culture helps explain why there is an absence of controversy over major issues even though factions exist on the board.

About half the agency representatives described themselves as playing facilitative roles on the board. They said they tried to be team members and to listen most of the time because minds were already made up and the more vocal members of the board, both agency and community representatives, dragged the meetings out too long anyway. Several said they consciously defended the community representatives when they felt they were being abused by agency people. One explained: "Instead of articulating my own thinking I'm trying to think what they are thinking and trying to interpret to the board what I think they are thinking in order that they might feel they are contributing." These facilitators were predominately the educators and lay people on the board, not the bureaucrats or the politicians.[50] The educators and lay people are in general also those who express the most distrust of the politicians and bureaucrats and of aggressive behavior on the board. None of the agency representatives explicitly said they played aggressive roles, but five did mention approaches in that general category. These mentioned playing devil's advocate,

questioning staff proposals, opposing theoretical solutions in favor
of practical solutions, and favoring rational planning as opposed to
mere response to political pressures.

In contrast with the agency representatives, two community
representatives did describe themselves as fighters involved in many
arguments on the board. Two community representatives who closely
identified with these fighters stressed the need for unity and for militancy, and indicated that they supported the two fighters. Two other
community representatives saw themselves as loners and one saw
himself as a facilitator between the agency people and the community people, trying to help EYOA avoid community controversy.
Consequently, while the community representatives had a higher
proportion of fighters (or supporters of fighters) than the agency
representatives, the overall board had a preponderance of facilitators.

The comments on roles illuminate the responses about the most
influential board members. The subjects had difficulty listing the
members they considered most influential. They qualified their responses by saying it was difficult to generalize, influence varied depending on the issue, and most of the members were about equal.
They stressed that EYOA was not the kind of board where one leader
has all the votes in his pocket. The absence of marked leadership was
attributed to the part-time aspect of the board, irregular attendance,
and the diverse backgrounds of the members. Observation suggests
another reason is the prevalence of facilitator roles and the con-
comitant distrust of aggressive board members, so the vocal members who might seem to be influential often have a negative effect.

Most agency representatives did mention the names of certain
individuals that came to their minds as influential.[51] The responses
support the members' comments about the even distribution of influence on the board. All agency representatives were mentioned at least
once and ten were mentioned once or twice.[52] So about half the agency representatives can be classified as having the reputation of some
influence, as shown in table 14. Seven individuals were mentioned
four or more times, which suggests they are more influential than the
others.[53] Yet none of these received more than eight mentions (which
is still less than half the board) and most got only four or five mentions. Influence does not appear highly concentrated but it is somewhat more concentrated in one half of the members than in the other.

It is noticeable that the seven individuals mentioned at least four times all come from different agencies. Each of the public agencies has one person who receives at least four mentions (these can be seen as the leader of each public agency delegation) and three of the private agencies do. None were Negroes or Mexican-Americans. The two individuals mentioned most often did not receive any negative

TABLE 14

Influential Members as Listed by the Agency Representatives

Number of mentions as influential	Number of agency representatives mentioned
0	0
1 or 2	10
4 or 5	4
6 or 7	2
8	1

mentions.[54] One was chosen because of his markedly nonaggressive style, described as fair, open, quiet, and wise by members who diverged widely on attitudes toward other aspects of EYOA. The other was listed because of his agency rather than his own role.

So far we have only considered agency representatives' comments on influential agency representatives. What did they say about influential community representatives? Only seven mentioned any community representatives in their lists of influential board members, and they qualified their mention by such phrases as, "of the community representatives." But when they were specifically asked who they saw as influential among the community representatives, there was wide consensus on one person. This representative had the strongest links to a community organization and the longest involvement with EYOA.

In summary, the responses on roles and influence on the board show that avoidance of controversy is valued. Controversy and conflict is minimized by the predominance of members who play facilitative roles and by the relatively even distribution of influence. Aggressive roles are antagonistic to the members. Value is placed on being cooperative. This internal culture of the board is consistent with EYOA's stress on service and the need for cooperation from the established agencies.[55] Yet it seems possible that this cooperative approach serves to limit the influence of community representatives on the board. It may inhibit free frank discussion of issues which would reveal the conflicting underlying interests involved.[56] The following sections of the chapter support this interpretation.

While the board culture helps explain the absence of controversy on important issues, the culture is only one factor. A more thorough analysis requires consideration again of the external relations of the board, first to the staff and then to the forces outside EYOA. This discussion of the lack of controversy will make it possible to formulate an answer to the major questions of this chapter: who has influence on the board, and what is the relative influence of the community representatives?

An important reason for the lack of controversy is the executive director's relationship to the board.[57] The director attempted to control the issues that came before the board, and all contact between the board and his staff.[58] The action that inevitably called forth his wrath was a board member trying to "meddle" with his staff.[59] His response in such a case was invariably, "If you don't have confidence in the executive director, get a new one, but don't interfere in my relationship with my staff." When a board member publicly questioned why an issue was presented to the board in a certain way, or why the staff acted in a certain manner, the issue quickly became one of the integrity of the director and the director had strong support.[60] So board members who had questions about an issue were reluctant to raise them publicly, though they might talk to the director privately, and when the issue came to a vote they might vote contrary to their own feelings on that issue because they felt it was more important to support the director.[61]

The activities of the executive director in revising the Joint Powers Agreement to comply with the Green amendment[62] provide an excellent example of how his control of the issues which came before the board contributed to the lack of controversy. The executive staff proposed changes in the Joint Powers Agreement which they said were necessary. Two of the four vacant seats created by the elimination of four public agency representatives would be filled by the ex-officio members of the board—the League of California Cities and the Chamber of Commerce. This left only two seats to be filled, and the proposal was that one Negro and one Mexican-American organization be chosen. Approval of these proposed changes was obtained not from the joint powers representatives on the board but from the top people in the public agencies.[63]

At the board meeting, discussion centered around how the two new organizations would be chosen. No one raised the issue of why the League and the Chamber should become members, and only one board member pointed out that the Green amendment would allow other types of changes in the board membership, such as an increase in community representatives, to fill the four vacant seats, but no other representatives followed this lead. The executive director had successfully prestructured the issue presented to the board to reduce controversy and was assured of the backing of the joint powers in case some controversy should arise.

The discussion of how the two new organizations were to be selected was settled in the same way most of the controversies on the board are settled, by referring it to a committee.[64] And since this was an issue which, like the election procedure, could arouse community passions, all the community representatives and only two joint powers representatives were put on the ad hoc committee, ostensibly because the community representatives knew more about minority organizations.[65] Presumably the joint powers, having been assured that two of the four new groups would be "safe" groups (the League of Cities and the Chamber), were not very concerned about the choice of the two minority groups and were glad to pass the onus of that decision to the community representatives (with the knowledge that if the Brown Berets and the Black Panthers were chosen, which was not likely, given the characteristics of the community representatives described in chapter 3, the joint powers could defeat the decision at the board level or refuse to approve the agreement when it came before the public agencies).

Before the ad hoc committee met, the staff had hit upon an ingenious technique for eliminating even the little controversy which it had originally allowed over which Negro and Mexican-American groups should be chosen. The executive staff had reread Green and found that it said the private sector of the community action agency boards should consist of "officials or members of business, industry, labor, religious, welfare, education, significant minority groups, and other major private groups and interests in the community." The staff then observed that the "major interests not represented in this group are industry, religious, and a major minority group in Los Angeles

County," the Orientals. The executive staff then proposed to the ad hoc committee that instead of picking a Negro or Mexican-American group, it would be more representative to pick the National Association of Manufacturers and an Oriental group (perhaps on a rotating basis with a Negro and a Mexican-American group).[66]

The committee consideration of this staff recommendation illustrated beautifully that the prestructuring of an issue determines the nature of the controversy. Seven community representatives were present for the committee meeting but the two appointed joint powers representatives were absent. The committee did not effectively question the staff assumption that since Negroes and Mexican-Americans were already represented on the board other groups should be selected. The debate centered on whether the committee should recommend that the board pick two groups from among the National Association of Manufacturers, Orientals, and Indians (the latter group was added by the committee to the staff recommendation) or that all three groups be chosen by the board. The first alternative was rejected by the committee because they felt the board would pick the National Association of Manufacturers and one minority group. The committee wanted to make sure both minority groups got on the board, yet still felt that the National Association of Manufacturers might find more jobs for poverty people if it was on the board, so the committee recommended that all three groups be added to the board and intended to leave the board the decision of which existing member would be dropped to make way for the extra group.

When the board refused to take all three groups (and to drop a current member from the board to keep the number at twenty-four) and picked instead the Oriental and Indian groups, the community representatives felt they had achieved a victory by getting the board to take both minority groups.[67] But actually it was the staff that had achieved a victory in the fight to minimize controversy.

The committee went along with the staff reasoning that since Negroes and Mexicans are on the board, no Negro and Mexican-American organizations need to be represented on the board. No one pointed out that using this reasoning, business and industry were already represented on the board since a board member was in private business in a large industry. One could also point out that the Chamber of Commerce had already been approved for membership and it represented many businesses and industries.[68] Note, too, that the committee went further in excluding consideration of the Negro and Mexican-American groups than even the staff had dared to go. The staff had proposed rotating membership among an Oriental, a Negro, and a Mexican group. The committee picked the Oriental group and did not discuss rotation.[69]

The reasons why the executive director and staff, by restructuring the issue, were able to successfully avoid heated controversy illustrate additional key features of the way the board functions. First, the members usually have less information on the issues than the staff. While the staff feels they do all they possibly can to supply board members with information in advance of board meetings, the agenda and meeting information get to board members only on the Saturday prior to the Monday meeting, which means they do not even have a chance to discuss them with co-workers until the morning of the board meeting. Many of the memoranda on key issues are not mailed out in advance, since the situation often changes hourly, but they are handed to the members when they go to the board meeting or are never actually presented in writing. Second, none of the board members gives as much time to board business as the staff. So even when they are provided with the information they often do not study it thoroughly or discuss it informally with other informed people. Accordingly, board members often have a low level of information about what is going on in board meetings and the implications of the various courses of action.[70] When these features of the board's operation are combined with a culture that stresses the value of avoiding controversy, the relative ease with which the board can be manipulated by the staff becomes apparent.[71]

The strong influence of the executive director and his staff on the board is further enhanced by the disjointed incrementalism and fragmentation of responsibility in EYOA's operation.[72] The committee system provides a vivid example. The committees are formally set up to make sure that some board members have given thorough consideration to matters coming before the board. But the committees rarely work out this way.

Very little probing of issues takes place at committee meetings. The agency representatives have a poor committee attendance record. Community representatives are in a majority at most committee meetings even though they do not make up a majority of the actual committee membership.[73] The result is that only certain sides of the issues are considered, those seen by the community representatives and the staff. The resulting committee recommendation is often not as thoroughly thought through as it might have been if more dialogue on the various perspectives had occurred.[74] This characteristic is heightened by variations in the staff approach to committee meetings. Sometimes the staff members present will be very directive, making a clear recommendation and defending it. At other times, they will not present recommendations or will present conflicting recommendations and then watch the committee come up with a recommendation. Then after the meeting they explain to the chairman why the recommendation must be modified.[75]

Haphazard consideration of issues in committees is just one of the characteristics of the committee system. Another is that the committees, like the board, are dependent on the staff for follow-through. Sometimes the committee recommendations are not clearly agreed upon by the whole committee. The result is that when the staff writes up what it thought was the recommendation, certain committee members feel the staff intentionally distorted the recommendation. At other times, the recommendation is clear but the staff modifies it to make it feasible, or at other times the staff just fails to carry it out. Further, the staff can be lax in setting up meetings of committees which are going in directions the staff does not like.

The major contribution to disjointed incrementalism comes in the articulation between committee action, staff action, and board action. Wide disagreement exists on the relative importance of each kind of action. Charges are often made that the committees and the board are simply rubber stamps for the staff. Observation of the committees shows that in about half the cases some changes are made in staff recommendations. For example, a staff recommendation that chairmen of committees be appointed by the chairman of the board is changed to provide for election of committee chairmen by the committee; a committee will not approve a staff report until the staff looks into the high rents being paid by certain delegate agencies for their offices; a committee modifies a staff proposal to require tabulation of the religion of children served by the Archdiocese's programs. But how significant are the changes? To an observer, most appear relatively minor, but to staff members committee changes seem more significant.[76]

What happens to committee recommendations when they get to the board? The executive office says that the committee's recommendations are usually accepted by the board (and this is cited as evidence of the influence of community representatives). Numerically this view is correct. But board members and other staff members point out that the board has learned that community representatives dominate the committees so that on important issues the committee recommendation "does not mean a thing." The conclusion of this observer is that the impact of committee recommendations depends upon the importance of the issue to the other board members. If they do not see the issue as important they will accept the committee as authoritative. If the issue is important to the agencies they represent, they will challenge unfavorable committee recommendations. But since many of the issues decided by committees are not seen as important and since value is placed on avoiding controversy, the board often appears to be rubber-stamping committees which in turn appear to be rubber-stamping the staff.

In sum, the disjointed incrementalism illustrated by the committee system helped strengthen the director's influence by fragmenting responsibility and providing a method for handling controversy. The director exercised discretion in referring business to committees. When an issue was urgent, he would present it directly to the board, but if opposition developed there, he suggested referring it to a committee to delay action and build up support. Or if an issue arose that he did not wish to decide himself, he passed the responsibility to the committees.[77] The director had significant influence over what committee got which issues and over the very membership of the committees. Committee assignments are carefully made by the staff to ensure that board members they see as troublemakers will not be on crucial committees.

The conclusion is that relations of the board to the staff help to account for the lack of controversy. The executive director carefully prestructured issues which came before the board, and the board members for a variety of reasons, such as the culture that stressed avoiding controversy and their lack of information, were not in a position to effectively question the actions. And the way that the internal proceedings of the board are carried out helps fragment responsibility and prevent thorough consideration of issues. This too avoids strong controversy on the board. The result is that the staff, and especially the executive director, has had a great deal of influence on the way the board functions.[78]

All the factors connected with the absence of controversy mentioned in the last two sections are not sufficient to explain the functioning of the board. Listing the factors, one begins to suspect there is an additional very basic factor that concerns the attitudes of the agency representatives toward EYOA. One reason so little questioning is done by the agency representatives seems to be that the agencies they represent are basically satisfied with EYOA, with the staff, and the programs.

The thesis here is that the agencies are satisfied with EYOA because they have enough influence on the operation of EYOA to ensure it does not conflict with their own interests. This does not mean that the agencies dictate all the actions of EYOA. The point is that the agencies in effect have a veto; on issues of concern to the agencies, no action can be taken to which the agencies strongly object.

The majority of both the public and private agencies are basically satisfied with EYOA,[79] but it is the public agencies that have the most influence. This influence is implied by the answers board members gave to a question about what forces outside the board have the most influence on the board. Even though the answers are generally vague and inconclusive, they focused on the issue of whether or not the public agencies ran the board. Those who denied that the public agencies ran the board insisted that no one group runs the board,[80] but they did not suggest the private agencies did. In fact, no one suggested that the private agencies ran the board, but many suggested the public agencies did. Those who said the public agencies did not run the board (and they were predominantly public agency people) gave some revealing explanations. For example, public agency representatives often stressed that the mayor did not run the board and actually leaned over backward to avoid manipulating it. When there were sit-ins or crises at EYOA they explained that the mayor would urge the executive director to do what he thought was right and assured him that his decisions would have the mayor's support. They pointed out the mayor never called the executive director and told him to hire certain people. These explanations suggest that the public agency people would not deny that the public agencies have a lot of influence; they are merely denying they have control in the sense of total control over all the operations of the board.[81]

The argument being made here is not that the public agencies completely run the board but merely that they have more influence on the board than the private agency or community representatives. The public agencies do use the board for their own interests when they want to.[82] EYOA took problems off the backs of the public agencies. Several board members pointed out how nice it is that when there are crises in the war on poverty the pickets go to EYOA rather than to city or county hall. Public agencies tend to take credit for EYOA's accomplishments but to say that criticism of EYOA should not be directed at the public agencies.[83] Thus the agencies are not interested in having complete control over EYOA. That is why they have not dictated decisions in certain crises or interfered in personnel matters. They do not care about many aspects of the board's functioning so have not chosen to exert influence in these areas. But on issues they care about, they do have predominant influence,[84] so they are basically satisfied with EYOA.

Though subjects mentioned both the schools and the city as public agencies that had the most influence on the board, the city was mentioned most often. The city was instrumental in developing the joint powers approach,[85] the city was in the forefront over the controversy about the merger of the Youth Opportunities Board (YOB) and the Economic Opportunity Federation, the city kept a top echelon official on the board longer than the county (the mayor's assistant was on for two and a half years, the county supervisor was on for one and a half years), and the city has supported EYOA more consistently than the county (note that in the spring of 1967 the county supervisors and the County Board of Education voted to bypass EYOA in negotiating Neighborhood Youth Corps contracts). As one board member pointed out, the city has the most influence not because of evil maneuvering, but because all board members understand that if the city is thwarted, it will pull out of EYOA. The special position of the city was illustrated best by a joke made at a board meeting considering funding for summer proposals. The largest single proposal, over $100,000, was a city proposal for a summer camp at Saugus. The chairman of the board, with obvious delight, moved that the proposal be defeated and joined in the general laughter that followed the motion. The implication was that everyone knew this proposal would be accepted by the board, as it actually was, because it was one the city wanted (as illustrated by the presence of the mayor's assistant who attends only when issues of special concern to the city are on the agenda).[86] A community representative said that if a community organization had turned in as poor a proposal as the city had, it would not have been accepted, but since the proposal came from the city, it was sent back for revision. Thus while descriptions of the Los Angeles political situation stress the relative powerlessness of the mayor in comparison with other mayors, the mayor appears relatively powerful in regard to EYOA.[87] And representatives of the mayor admit that the mayor saw the creation of YOB and EYOA as a way for the city to get more voice in the handling of social problems than it had had. YOB and EYOA, both cutting across jurisdictional lines, helped centralize government and thus strengthen the influence of the mayor's office.[88]

The above picture of the predominant influence of the public agencies on EYOA and its board emerges from interviews and observation. When applied to EYOA neither the reputational nor the decisional approaches to influence provide entirely satisfactory results. The board members' responses about external influences do not show a clear consensus. Some said the public agencies did not have dominant influence, others said they did. And analysis of who wins the important controversial decisions is hampered by the fact that most of the important issues are not controversial and the board members were vague about how the important decisions were made. An impressionistic adaptation of these two approaches to the arena of poverty decisions in Los Angeles suggests that the public agencies dominate.

One wishes that there were clearer examples of that public influence, examples of A telling B to do C or else. But the influence at EYOA does not fit the conspiratorial model of a powerful elite pulling strings behind the scenes.[89] It does bear resemblance to the pluralist model insofar as the governmental officials are important to the decisions.[90] And it also resembles Barach and Baratz's notion of the "other face of power"; they point out that the absence of controversial decisions can be indicative of power just as much as the winning of a controversial issue.[91]

The decisional method reveals that the public representatives are on the winning side of issues which come before the board more often than the other representatives. And when an issue is important to them a majority vote together and have the private agency representatives as allies. Thus they have primary influence on the votes they are concerned with.[92] But because of the absence of controversial issues this does not adequately indicate the way the public agencies exert their influence. Their influence does not need to be explicitly exerted. As board members said, "It is understood." It is a fact of life to board members that if the interests of the public agencies are not being met by EYOA they will not cooperate. The underlying assumption is that in Los Angeles, where public agencies play a relatively major role in social services, no poverty program can be effective without the cooperation of the public agencies. So, in order to get their cooperation, the board, the executive director, and his staff must consider their interests.[93] This fact lies behind the absence of controversy on the board. We have seen how the executive director prestructured issues that came before the board to avoid controversy; this prestructuring is satisfactory to the public agencies because they know it has taken their interests into account. Thus their implicit influence helps control the way issues come before the board and limits the conflict on those issues. Some charge that this type of influence is a nonevent and is therefore by definition nonempirical[94] but the mistake is the label "nonevent." Something *is* happening. It is not nothing; it is a subtle event, an elusive process. This study of EYOA suggests that Barach and Baratz are correct in urging social scientists to give more attention to describing what *is* happening.[95]

Study of EYOA also illustrates the proposition that the prevailing forces in a community capture new programs.[96] And if the prevailing forces set up the kind of organization they want and select a significant portion of the members of the board and the executive director they want, they will not need to be involved in the day-to-day decisions that are made.[97] The result of this kind of prestructuring and preselection is that the participants on the board may not be aware of the influences at work.[98] Another reason why the board members are not aware of the way in which the agencies exert influence is that the consultations that take place do not ordinarily take place between the executive director and the board members from the public agencies. Instead, the discussions are between the executive director and the higher echelon people in the public agencies. The top people often do not inform the board members that the consultation has taken place or give explicit directions to their board members on how to vote. But the prior consultation assures the executive director that he will have the support of the joint powers in the event that a controversy does arise.[99]

INFLUENCE OF THE COMMUNITY REPRESENTATIVES

The preceding discussion of the predominance of the public agencies' influence on the board leads to the conclusion that the community representatives do not have as much power on the board as the public representatives. The argument here is that the community representatives have been formally co-opted. The term co-optation has been vulgarized and is often used whenever somebody does something we do not like. But it refers here to what Selznick calls "the process of absorbing new elements into the leadership or policy-determining structure of the organization as a means of averting threats to its stability or existence."[100] Formal co-optation is when this absorption occurs without any change in the distribution of power. This study of EYOA shows, as the literature leads us to expect, that the community representatives have been absorbed into EYOA's board without any actual redistribution of power taking place. They have been asked to share in carrying the burdens and responsibilities rather than in exercising the power of the board.

The most obvious indicator of formal co-optation is that the community representatives have only eight votes and the agency representatives sixteen. So even if the community representatives did vote together, they would not be able to outvote the agency representatives. Theoretically, the community representatives could gain the private agency representatives as allies, but actually the private agencies vote more often with the public representatives. And the community representatives usually are divided so they do not actually use the voting power they formally have. This division helps explain why the joint powers have not objected to the steady decrease of their relative number of votes on the board.

Remember that originally the joint powers fought fiercely to ensure that they would have 51 percent of the board membership. They clearly thought that the formal voting strength would reflect informal power and they were determined to have a preponderance of power. When the federal guidelines were changed to require that community representatives make up a third of community action agency boards, however, the joint powers did not object when the number of community representatives was increased from seven to eight, even though this left the joint powers with only 50 percent of the board membership. Why no objections? Interviews revealed that the joint powers had found out that formal voting strength did not reflect informal power; they could still have predominant influence on the board even though they did not have 51 percent of the votes. They discovered that the community representatives did not vote together, the private agency representatives were often allies of the joint powers, and the interests of the joint powers were not effectively challenged by the community representatives. This same reasoning explains why the joint powers did not object when their voting strength was decreased from twelve to eight as a result of the Green amendment. The joint powers are clearly confident that their predominant power will not be threatened.

Selznick suggests several methods for locating actual control over citizen groups that may have been co-opted.[101] Even though the tests were designed to apply to committees and not to governing bodies like EYOA, they can be adapted to it. The prime test is whether approach to the group by outside elements is channeled through officials of the co-opting agency. As discussed in the section on representation, EYOA community representatives are constantly urged by the staff, agency representatives, and even other community representatives, to refer all complaints they get to the staff and not become an advocate of any outside group. Thus while contacts with the community representatives do not have to be channeled through EYOA staff, a similar effect may be achieved by channeling community representatives' actions through the staff. Another test Selznick applies is whether the groups are linked with the network of community organization or whether they are tools used by the staff, thus relieving the staff of official responsibility for its actions without actually gaining control of activities. Again, the community representatives would appear to be co-opted. As discussed above, the system of electing community representatives and their notions of who they should represent work against their developing ties with community organizations. And the community representatives do appear to be tools utilized sometimes by the staff, sometimes by other board members. Even though they do interact more than the agency representatives they do not succeed in doing effective pre-planning of the strategies they will follow in meetings. This reflects partly their lack of experience in such maneuvers, but shows more importantly their lack of a power base.

The community representatives are aware that they do not have predominant influence on the board, and it is a source of constant frustration to many of them. One said that "people laugh at us and say we are just puppets helping the professionals justify putting money in their own pockets." Cloward says: "Membership on policy making bodies may confer a little prestige on the poor persons who participate, but it will do little more than that when they are outnumbered by the representatives of organizational interests. Indeed, having been granted representation on city-wide antipoverty councils, they now seem vaguely uneasy about their victory. They begin to sense they have been victorious on the wrong battlefield or a relatively nostrategic one."[102] The community representatives' sensitivity to charges of being rubber stamps for the establishment suggest that they share this uneasiness.

The findings of this study support Kenneth Clark's position that the poor on boards are not influential or taken seriously in any major decision. He says: "Generally the poor serving on community action boards have proved vulnerable to blandishments and have been easily absorbed or controlled, or flattered. They are permitted to blow off steam; a proportion of agenda time is, as it were, allocated to group therapy. . . . But it seldom affects the outcome of policy."[103] It is true that using indicators such as service on committees and as committee chairmen, and information on board agendas, the community representatives appear to participate as actively on the board as the other members.[104] The fact remains, however, that their influence is not equal to that of the other participants. The community representatives are useful to EYOA, for they explain EYOA to the community and serve as calming agents; they help take the responsibility off the staff and the other board members. But all this is subject to the willingness of the public agencies, and the agencies will not permit the community representatives to gain predominant power on the board.

This description of how the influence patterns at EYOA help explain the lack of controversy and the lack of power among the community representatives does not explain why more controversy has not arisen in the poverty community over the war on poverty. Why have poor people not been more effective in protesting the predomi-

nant power of the public agencies on EYOA? Why was there no protest when plans for area councils were discarded? Why no outcry
when Negro and Mexican-American organizations were bypassed in
filling the four vacancies on the board?

It is possible to point to such factors as the fragmentation of the
power structure in Los Angeles, the absence of a strongly centralized
organization to fight against, the weakness of political parties, and
traditional low participation. But protest of various kinds does arise
from time to time in Los Angeles: witness the Anti-Poverty Committee (which loudly objected to the joint powers attempts to control the
original structure of EYOA), the Black Congress, and the organized
objections to police performance and school programs. So the question is why have major protest organizations not focused on EYOA?
Board members will point out that many groups have come to board
meeting with hostile protests.[105] But these groups have predominantly
been part of poverty programs with specific grievances about funding
or personnel.[106] They may refer bitterly to the overall power structure
of EYOA, but they are not organized to change that. After attempts
are made by the board to placate their specific grievances, they dis-
appear, disgruntled perhaps, but deactivated.

In Los Angeles there are no organized groups pushing for more
grass roots community organization to fight the joint powers' grip on
the poverty program. One explanation is that the militant groups that
could make this their focus just do not care about the poverty program. They see it as institutionalized, predetermined, and as not important enough to try to change—as not where the action is.[107] It is
interesting to speculate how much of this lack of concern is the result
of successful attempts by the public agencies to ensure that no effective grass roots organizations ever did threaten the poverty program
in Los Angeles. The handling of the election system for community
representatives, the area councils, and the Neighborhood Adult Participation Project all suggest this possibility. There are stories that the
major intervened to force the cutoff of federal funds to area councils
and to ensure that the Neighborhood Adult Participation Project
would be divested and become more of a manpower program than a
community organization program. But whatever the pressures were,
whether local or national, from the mayor or from congressmen, the
result is that Los Angeles has not developed strong community-action
oriented groups focusing on the poverty program.[108] And it does not

seem likely that the war on poverty will become a focus of controversy unless these pressures change.

To review, the data presented in this chapter on the functioning of the EYOA indicates that the community representatives have been co-opted; their presence has not redistributed power. This conclusion is supported by evidence that the representational roles of community representatives are conceived of differently from the agency representatives' roles. It is also indicated by the presence on controversial issues of a faction of at least half the community representatives which is on the losing side. The absence of controversy on key issues is also an indication of co-optation. The lack of controversy results partly from the internal culture of the board which places value on cooperative members, and partly from the strong influence of the executive director and staff over the board and their skill at taking into account the interests of the public agencies which have predominant influence on the board. The community representatives have been able to influence the outcome of issues only when the agencies do not object. To say that the community representatives are not predominant, or have not redistributed power, does not necessarily mean that they have not had any effect at all on the board. Clark and Cloward imply that the presence of community representatives is totally useless for change; that the effects have been totally negative. The following chapter on the attitudes of board members attempts to suggest some of the positive effects they have had on it.

5. The Board's Effect on the Attitudes of Its Members

Discussions of the war on poverty often end with considerations of who has predominant influence. When the conclusion is that the poor have not redistributed power, it may appear that maximum feasible participation is a complete failure, that social reform is not possible because the powerful forces remain powerful. However, the present study assumes that the small-scale flexibilities in a system can provide an important basis for larger changes. This assumption is based on Wilbert Moore's formulation that large-scale social change is the result of both the flexibilities and uncertainties inherent in all social systems and the existence of environmental and social challenges.[1] Thus this research looks at small changes taking place among the participants in the community action experiment; it looks at the socialization of EYOA board members. What is happening to them as a result of being on the board? Just because the community representatives have not shared in the power of the public agencies on the board does not mean that their participation is meaningless. The process must be looked at as well as the product. The process, by changing communication patterns, may change people's attitudes.[2]

The effect of maximum feasible participation on attitudes has been largely ignored, even by educators who presumably would be most interested in such changes in attitudes. Ideological reasons may help explain why attitude changes in the poverty program have been ignored. Social scientists are certainly aware that these changes are taking place[3] but they may want to maintain a radical posture and fear that attention to attitudes will weaken their demands and make them seem to be accommodationists. The neglect may also be part of

the lack of interest in the whole realm of adult socialization. Social
scientists interested in learning tend to focus on childhood socialization. Even sociologists who stress the influence of situational factors
on human personality tend to view changes in adults as very superficial. Yet some existing work on adult socialization suggests that important changes in attitudes do take place later in life.[4]

The literature on adult socialization suggests a variety of variables which may influence adult socialization.[5] The ones most relevant here are: (a) prior personal socialization, (b) organizational
position, (c) roles played in the group, and (d) the nature of the
socializing agent. EYOA, viewed as a socializing agent, is a formal
organization in which learning takes place by trial and error. This is
typical of much of adult socialization. One would expect that (a),
(b), and (c), act as a perceptual screen for the stimuli.[6] Some literature suggests that organizational role is more important than background in determining what is learned.[7] On the other hand, when a
situation is ambiguous, personality appears to affect behavior independent of role.[8]

This chapter considers the attitudes and changes in attitude
described by EYOA board members in taped interviews. The respondents are those who were on the board before the election of the new
community representatives in March 1968; the attitudes of the newly
elected community representatives are the subject of the chapter
which follows. The first two sections of this chapter talk about board
members' attitudes toward community representatives, their effect
and their presence. The following sections discuss members' attitudes
toward EYOA and its staff. The final sections focus directly on
changes in attitudes, including political attitudes.

OPINIONS ABOUT THE EFFECT OF COMMUNITY
REPRESENTATIVES ON THE BOARD

Even though the preceding analysis suggests that community
representatives have been co-opted and have not gained predominant
power on the board, approximately two-thirds of all the board members stated that the community representatives had influenced the
board. This degree of consensus was reflected in the answers of both
the agency representatives and the community representatives.[9] An
examination of the types of influence the subjects had in mind helps

explain the discrepancy and the reason why co-optation does not negate the possibility that the community representatives are having certain effects on the board.

The agency people who responded positively cited several different types of influence. One type often referred to was a general influence on the thinking and feelings of the agency people. Statements were made that the agency representatives have seen a point of view which they may have known about, but they have seen it differently because of the personal comments and anecdotal case histories given by the community representatives.[10] One commented: "I think I did know poverty, but I didn't know there were four year old kids that didn't know this was their elbow, and didn't really know their name was George. This to me is the most appalling thing I've run into." Another agency representative stated: "The continuing witness of what the poverty representatives are saying has, without the power structure knowing it, altered their point of view." The alteration was described as leading to more tolerance, more understanding of the needs and problems of poverty.

Another example of influence often given by the agency people was the provision of information on the details behind projects. Community representatives were said to look into projects from a different viewpoint than either the staff or the other board members. One respondent said: "When you read a proposal it sounds good, but you are not aware of the real practical facts that occur in the operation of the program. I go down there and go through programs . . . big shot on the board, and they give me a regular tour. The big whitewash. The community representatives can go down and really find out. They hear from their neighbors." Community representatives were credited with focusing attention on possible irregularities in various projects.[11]

When the agency representatives were asked for examples of specific board decisions which the community representatives influenced, they tended to have some difficulty (but they pointed out they would also have difficulty giving examples of board decisions influenced by the agency representatives). Examples mentioned were the location and retention of certain projects, the per diem reimbursement of community representatives, and increased employment of indigenous people in EYOA projects. Several agency representatives pointed out that these actions would have occurred whether or not the community representatives were there, but others said that since the community representatives pushed for them they happened faster. A final example of influence by community representatives could be called influence based on deference. Many of the agency representatives stressed that the agency people feel they ought to try to go along with what the community representatives wanted because "we don't want to give them the feeling that we're opposed unless it's an outrageous thing."

Since the agency representatives might be reluctant to bring up the negative effects of community representatives, the interview specifically probed for these. The most widely mentioned one was that the community representatives made the meetings very long. Agency representatives also stressed the problems in communication. Comments were made that "community representatives just don't know how to play the game of board membership." The addition of community representatives was described as a very painful process because agency people over a period of time learn to talk the same language but they had to learn a new language and try to build up a sense of trust between community people and agency people.[12]

Closely related to the often-mentioned problems of communication and time was the problem of what the agency representatives called the emotional hang-ups of the community representatives. The agency representatives said that many things which seemed trivial to them were important to the community representatives. One subject said the community representatives think with their blinkers on and do not relate the problems they see to other priorities.[13]

The five community representatives who felt they had had influence cited examples of influence similar to those mentioned by the agency representatives. Several cited influence on the thinking and consciences of the agency representatives. One said: "I do think we changed some of their minds. At first they were kind of nasty with us but over two years their attitudes changed." Early incidents were mentioned when agency representatives said to community representatives, "we don't have to sit here and discuss with you people," and "you are ignorant," but such comments have ceased.

Three of the five community representatives who said the representatives did have influence stressed, however, that the influence was "very, very small compared to the others."[14] And two community representatives chose to stress the lack of influence of the community representatives. One said "our effectiveness was none"; the other stated that the agency people were very hostile, "if they could see we were really going for something they would always go against us."

It is difficult to assess the influence indicated by these results. One suspects that all respondents, if guided by the questioner, would have acknowledged that the community representatives had had an effect on the functioning of the board to some degree. Rossi and Dentler include a cogent discussion of the difficulty of knowing what standard to apply in evaluating the effectiveness of community organization.[15] The same difficulties arise in evaluating the effect of community representatives. It is already clear from the preceding chapter that community representatives do not have predominant power. They have not had significant impact on the major decisions of the board. But the comments of the subjects suggest that the community representatives have had some effect on the decisions of the board. Observations confirm that the community representatives did effect the decisions listed by the respondents.[16] Comments by community representatives in committees do lead to certain revisions in staff proposals and committee recommendations are often acceptable to the board. But in all these cases the community representatives' ideas are acceptable to other board members. In other words, the community representatives have had some influence when the agency representatives are willing to be influenced. On issues that are not of major concern to the agency representatives there is leeway.

For those who are interested in a redistribution of power, the marginal effect of the EYOA community representatives is unsatisfactory since it depends totally on the willingness of the power holders to be influenced. But it is argued here that the presence of community representatives has value because they speak for interests that are different from those of the public agencies. It is true that they prevail only in a limited number of relatively unimportant issues, but without the community representatives even these issues might have been decided differently. And even on issues where the majority of community representatives are on the losing side, their comments serve to underline a viewpoint that might not otherwise have been expressed.[17]

Both the agency representatives and the community representatives stressed this educational effect of the community representatives on the board. Several community representatives said that the power to advise was at least a step toward the power to decide. On a board marked by an absence of controversy and questioning, the community representatives are more likely to play the role of questioners than the other representatives. They ask why the established agencies do not use more of their own funds to provide programs for the poor rather than relying on federal funds; why the staff is not franker about shortcomings of programs; and why action has not been taken to correct problems.

ATTITUDE TOWARD COMMUNITY REPRESENTATIVES
BEING ON THE BOARD

In order to determine what effect the questions and comments of the community representatives have had on the other board members' evaluation of community representatives, the agency representatives were asked whether they favored having community representatives on the board. When this research was being designed several people warned ominously that board members would never admit their negative feelings about the inclusion of community representatives. But the respondents did reveal both negative and positive attitudes toward community representatives.

The same five board members who felt that the community representatives had had little significant influence on the board showed negative or ambivalent attitudes toward their presence, feeling that the community representatives did not make any positive contributions to the board because of their lack of leadership experience. Several said their inclusion was a solely political move to quiet the demands from poverty people for power. One agency representative, explaining why community representatives were added, said: "Nobody was very serious about it. We all know that. Just a massive exercise in hypocrisy. . . . Everyone was conning everyone."

Three of the agency representatives, who stated that the community representatives had influenced the board, had mixed feelings about their presence on the board. Two of them said at first they thought the decision to include them was not wise. But they said the presence of community representatives had shown they could make certain limited contributions to the board; community representatives were often the best committee members, attending most regularly and being most prepared often with firsthand information they had gathered on the topic to be discussed.

Two agency representatives who were enthusiastic about the participation of community representatives also indicated that their attitudes toward community representatives had become more positive after watching them on the board. One respondent said: "In the back of my mind I thought, these are community people and they really should be involved, but I wasn't really convinced they could know what we were talking about, and they didn't for a long, long time. But they sure caught on fast. I have nothing but admiration for them." Seven other agency representatives expressed enthusiasm for the inclusion of community representatives.

Thus if the expressed attitudes are added together, one finds that eight agency representatives were either ambivalent or negative and nine felt positively about the inclusion of community representatives.[18] The responses suggest two main types of reasons for favoring participation by poor people. One stresses the education and therapy the board provides to the representative. The other stresses the contributions the representatives make to the board. These contributions may be of two types. One consists of influencing the board's deliberations by communications to the board about the needs and attitudes in the community. The other consists of building public confidence in the board by communicating and explaining the board's deliberations.[19] A third major reason for favoring the involvement of community representatives did not come out very clearly in the interviews, but several subjects implied that community people ought to have some say about what goes on in their communities. This reason may be independent of whether or not the community representatives really know what is best for them, or whether they make a contribution to the board. It is an argument for participation in the process, for inclusion in the arena in which the struggle is going on. It may be an ethical argument—that human beings have a right to participate —or it may be a strategy for obtaining a given decision outcome, such as a change in an established institution.

But for a variety of reasons, the presence of community representatives has been influential in changing the attitudes of at least four agency people, so that they feel more positively toward inclusion of the poor. And those who said they always favored the idea may have been reinforced in their attitudes. Conversely, no agency person had changed from positive feelings to negative feelings, although several people who felt negatively in the beginning may have had their attitudes reinforced.

ATTITUDES TOWARD EYOA AND THE WAR
ON POVERTY

Splits in the attitudes toward EYOA exist among both the agency representatives and the community representatives; in both groups positive attitudes and negative attitudes were expressed. As might be expected, a larger percentage of agency representatives than community representatives said they were favorable.[20] The splits suggest the danger of generalizations that all agency representatives support EYOA or that all the community representatives have been bought off by the establishment and now support EYOA.

The agency representatives had varied reasons for negative feelings toward EYOA. The reasons given included: opposition to governmental domination and the bypassing of established voluntary agencies; the inefficiency of EYOA compared with established local governments; EYOA's ineffectiveness as an agent of change in the established bureaucracies; and disillusionment with the resurgence of vested political interests. Several respondents commented that EYOA is a "faceless intermediary" which receives and disburses money but has no mind of its own, merely accommodating existing forces.[21] One can speculate that all the above representatives who currently express negative feelings toward EYOA would rally to its support if the alternative to EYOA were increased governmental control from either the state or federal level.[22]

The five community representatives who expressed negative feelings toward EYOA agreed on the reasons for their feelings. While they acknowledged that some individuals on the board seemed sincerely interested in eliminating poverty and that some agencies had made efforts, the community representatives felt that these individuals could not do enough, that they are trapped by the system and the system is hostile to the needs of the poor.[23] Each of the community representatives who expressed negative attitudes toward EYOA pointed to some good results, but on balance they still felt that nothing really worthwhile had been accomplished, nothing that was really going to change things.[24] One said: "The poor won't ever really have a chance to get out of poverty. They will give you a hand so you can straighten up a little but they don't really want you to be on your two feet." These feelings suggest that while some agency representatives and community representatives are allied in negative feelings to EYOA (7 plus 5, or a total of 12 votes, not enough to pass a measure but sufficient to prevent motions from passing depending on which representatives are present at a particular meeting), they would find it difficult to agree on an alternative to EYOA.

Splits also exist among board members' attitudes toward the EYOA staff. Certain agency and community representatives frequently questioned reports made to the board by the executive director and staff. These representatives made comments that they had not gotten information far enough ahead of the meeting, or they thought more information was needed or that the staff ought to look into aspects that had been overlooked.

Four agency representatives expressed negative feelings toward both the staff and the executive director. They said they questioned the staff because it had too much control over the board and said the director had the board in his pocket. At the other extreme, five agency representatives expressed faith in the staff and executive director and a willingness to go along with their recommendations. The middle group is most interesting because it is composed of four people who expressed negative feelings about the director's staff but very positive support of the executive director.[25]

The reasons given by agency representatives for negative feelings toward the staff and the executive director were predictably varied and contradictory. Some viewed the staff as incompetent. They said it is very hard to get qualified people to work for a new, insecurely established type of organization such as EYOA, and it therefore tends to attract those who were not successful in the established organizations, "the residue." Others said the staff is too concerned with sociological theory and not practical enough.[26] Others said just the opposite, that the staff was too concerned with action at the expense of conceptual planning. Similarly some felt the executive director was too dictatorial and others commented that he gave in to pressures too much, trying to dance too many ways at once, and thus avoided making some decisions that needed to be made, such as the changing of subcontractors.

While approximately the same number of agency representatives expressed negative attitudes toward EYOA and toward the staff, more community representatives expressed hostility toward EYOA than expressed hostility toward the staff.[27] Some of the community representatives who felt negatively toward EYOA trusted the EYOA staff. One explained, "As they got to know us and that we were trying to be sincere and wanting really good programs, then they began to tell us if a thing wasn't right; before they were just wishy washy, beat around the bush. They found out they could trust us and us them." The five who expressed positive feelings toward the director said that he was trying to be fair and that he had to be dictatorial in order to run such a big program.

The preponderance of trust expressed toward the staff by the community representatives is interesting because they often complained during meetings of various irregularities in EYOA programs and would cite specific examples where they felt the EYOA staff did not tell the truth or provide enough information. They had potential allies for this position among some of the joint powers representatives. Several community representatives indicated an awareness of this by commending certain joint powers representatives who "don't let things get by." In general, however, the community representatives expressed more trust of EYOA personnel than of the public agencies.

Even though the above description of attitudes toward EYOA indicates differences in the representatives' evaluations, the interviews suggested that there is widespread agreement on specific strengths and weaknesses. The major disagreements are over how the specific accomplishments should be weighted and what the standard of comparison ought to be. In other words, some said that the accomplishments were great compared with the accomplishments of other organizations. Others said the accomplishments fall far short of what they could have been or ought to have been.

The accomplishments of EYOA which were mentioned most often included: making the community more aware of poverty, doing some good for poor people once the money finally gets down to them, bringing together the major governmental units in a program that is closer to the people than any one of the units would have been on its own, and stimulating leadership among poverty people. One agency representative explained: "I see people who two years ago were so afraid they would never get before a public and speak. Now, a lot of times they are not on the subject or making themselves known by the required standards, but they are speaking and that is the main thing."

The most frequent criticism of Los Angeles' war on poverty concerned the politics involved and the federal activities. Negative comments were made on federal regulation changes, unrealistic deadlines resulting in rushed decisions, budget cuts that disillusioned local people, and interdepartmental power struggles between Labor, OEO, and Congress which prevented local coordination. These comments challenge Grodzins' notion of cooperative federalism.[28] There is undoubtedly interpenetration in the poverty program, but rather than being cooperative it appears to be marked by distrust and competition.

All agency representatives regardless of their evaluation of EYOA were asked what effect EYOA had had on their agencies, what institutional changes it had stimulated. Only a few subjects saw this as a purpose of EYOA. Many respondents said that the federal dollars made agencies pay attention to the people with problems and planted the idea that change in established ways of doing things was required.[29] EYOA and poverty money were also seen as a stimulus for specific new programs which had previously been resisted, such as the use of nonprofessional aides in schools and social agencies.[30] Partly as a result of such programs civil service procedures are being reevaluated. The subjects pointed out, however, that by and large the agencies have not adopted programs developed by EYOA as their own programs, budgeted out of their own funds.[31]

Members' comments are consistent with three generalizations made by Marris and Rein about the effect of the community action programs on established institutions. They suggest that the community action programs had (a) set new criteria of performance for public and private social agencies, namely imaginative service to the poor; (b) redistributed resources; and (c) breached the old divisions between public and private and between various levels of government.[32] A fourth generalization made by Marris and Rein is particularly interesting for this study. They suggest that community action programs have created the professional reformer who is a new kind of public servant, more independent of established authority and more responsive to the people. None of the EYOA board members indicated that they had seen this development within their own agencies and they did not talk as if they saw themselves in this role. To see whether this generalization applies to Los Angeles, one would probably have to look at the EYOA staff itself. Indications are that the EYOA staff is more oriented toward institutional change and organizing the poor than the EYOA board. It might be on the EYOA staff that one could find the new kind of public servant.

What conclusions can be drawn from the above description of board members' attitudes toward EYOA? First, the discussion in the preceding chapter about the absence of controversy on the board, and the general support of the joint powers agencies for the board, must be tempered somewhat by the fact that certain board members do feel suspicious toward either the staff or EYOA or both. While the agency representatives in general support both EYOA and its staff, some agency representatives do not, even though their agencies do. Thus there are agency representatives who do create some limited controversy on the board. Second, the interview underscored the board members' lack of concern with and clarity about the goals of EYOA. Just as little attention has been given to the roles of board members, the formulation of goals has been largely ignored. Third, the community representatives have apparently not been won over by the board. They may have been co-opted but they have not been brainwashed. The literature on the war on poverty leads one to expect that the poverty representatives will switch from their local orientation to a downtown orientation, and that, like union shop stewards, they will learn to behave like their social betters and lose the characteristics of those they represent.[33] This possibility will be discussed later in this chapter, but at least in regard to their attitudes toward EYOA the community representatives did not become more positive toward EYOA. Even though many of the agency representatives indicated that they had become more tolerant of community representatives, the community representatives had not become more tolerant of EYOA.

So far this chapter has discussed the attitudes of board members toward community representatives and EYOA, without directly focusing on changes in attitude. The rest of the chapter treats changes in attitudes, first in the agency representatives and then in the community representatives.

CHANGES IN THE ATTITUDES OF THE
AGENCY REPRESENTATIVES

Responses about attitude change must be used cautiously. Retrospective recall has limited reliability as an indicator of objective change in attitudes,[34] but it is a valuable indicator of what people think the changes in their attitudes have been. Both agency representatives and community representatives stressed that the experience of being on the board had been very trying personally. They described the experience as painful and difficult, and said they had thought of quitting numerous times.

The most frequently cited change in attitude among agency representatives was an increase in tolerance for the community people's points of view and in understanding of the problems of poverty. Eleven agency representatives talked about this kind of change. Many specifically said the community representatives were responsible for this change. One agency representative explained: "At the beginning I remember very vividly having lunch with one or two of them and one of them turned to me and said you just don't know how it is to have to worry about washing machine payments and getting money together to buy food for the children." Another stated: "At first I was not tolerant of their lack of experience and I more or less abused them only because I thought they should have known as much as I did. But the poor have taught me to have more patience. It was an education to me." Four community representatives said that they too had seen a change in the agency representatives toward more understanding.

Turning to other types of changes in attitudes among agency representatives, three kinds of changes were mentioned about equally. All of them relate to the EYOA program itself. Four subjects specifically described changes in their attitudes toward the program. Three of these said their attitude had become more positive and one said he felt more negative. Some who did not say that their attitude to EYOA had changed nevertheless added that they had become discouraged and no longer had their original fight because their efforts kept getting slapped down, mainly because of the national climate.

Four subjects referred to changes in their own representational role on the EYOA board.[35] Two said that when they first went on they were primarily concerned with the interests of their own agency but that gradually their perspective broadened and they became concerned with the bigger picture—that is, with the interests of the community. But two others reported the reverse. The broadened perspective apparently developed because the agency those men represented was under the least attack from the rest of the board. If attacks had occurred they would have had to speak more often from the viewpoint of their agency.

Four subjects referred to changes in their understanding of EYOA and social action. Three of them specifically said they had become less naïve and more realistic and went on to describe an increasing awareness of the political interests involved, the power game. One subject described a change in the opposite direction; he said that at first he was wondering what axes the other representatives had to grind but that now he trusts them more.

The preceding section summarizes changes that the subjects themselves mentioned in response to general questions about changes in their own attitudes. Other attitude changes were revealed by further specific questions. The resulting findings on attitudes toward federal involvement in the poverty program, militancy, and liberalism and conservatism are rather fuzzy. Often it was not clear to what extent the subjects thought their attitudes had changed. But from their comments a general picture of their thinking does emerge.

All agency representatives in talking about the federal government expressed negative feelings toward the lack of money available for the poverty program, the lack of responsiveness to local needs, and so on. Five of the agency representatives spoke strongly of the need for continued and increased federal leadership, however, and indicated that they had always felt this need. Their positive feelings toward the national government were intensified by their experience with EYOA. On the other hand, eight subjects talked as if their prior suspicion of the federal government had been reinforced by EYOA. Only one subject stated that his prior positive evaluation of the federal government had completely changed to a negative picture. He said that he used to think the federal government was God but now he views it as a "menace" because "they don't know what they are doing and yet they are very rigid." He added that "they send people out here to make pronouncements and they honestly don't know what they are talking about." He said that five years ago he welcomed all federal grants but now is immediately suspicious and would go so far as to say give the money to the states and "let us run our own show."[36]

The agency representatives' responses about their attitudes toward militancy show a preponderance of negative reactions.[37] Eight of the agency representatives indicated that they felt negatively toward militancy. Responses included the following: threats make me go the other way, militants are paid troublemakers who only understand rough treatment, Negro leaders are trying to push for change too hard, the pendulum has swung too far so that stress is now on change even if we have to destroy the thing we are trying to change. Two subjects specifically mentioned increased acceptance of militancy.

Agency representatives were also asked whether they thought of themselves as liberals or conservatives. The political party identification of the respondents shows twelve registered Democrats, four registered Republicans, and one who declined to register in either party.[38] The twelve registered Democrats picked the term liberal rather than conservative, but then six of these went on to qualify the term to indicate that they see themselves as middle-of-the-road. For example, one said he is getting more conservative with age, and less impressed with social action. Another said he is conservative when it comes to rate of change and is one of the few people who calls himself a liberal who views militant movements as linked with communist-party type movements. Only two respondents said involvement with EYOA had changed their political ideology; these two said they grew more liberal as they became increasingly aware of the need for change.

Just as half the registered Democrats see themselves as middle-of-the-road, half the registered Republicans see themselves as moderate. Only one of the moderate Republicans mentioned a change; he said that he has become more positive toward the use of federal funds to fight poverty.

The data indicate that the agency representatives experienced both resocialization and reinforcement of prior socialization while they were on the EYOA board. As shown in table 15, the agency representatives are split in their attitudes toward EYOA, the federal government, militancy, and liberalism and their attitudes changed in different directions. On most issues there are representatives who mention becoming more hostile and becoming less hostile (see table 16). The major exception to this split occurs on the issue of attitude toward community representatives. On this topic the responses indicate a predominant trend toward more understanding and acceptance of community representatives. Thus, while contact with EYOA has not uniformly influenced political attitudes such as liberalism, it has made attitudes toward community representatives more positive.

TABLE 15

Attitudes of the Agency Representatives after Being on the Board

Attitude toward	Positive	Negative	No answer
Community representatives	9	8	0
EYOA	10	7	0
Executive director	9	4	4
Staff	5	8	4
Federal government	5	8	3
Militancy	6	8	3
Liberal Democrat self-image	6	6	
Liberal Republican self-image	2	2	

TABLE 16

Changes in Attitudes of Agency Representatives

Attitude toward	Changes in positive direction	Changes in negative direction
Community representatives being on the board	4	0
Community point of view	11	0
EYOA	3	1
Federal government	5	8
Militancy	1	1
Liberal Democrat self-image	2	1
Liberal Republican self-image	1	0

A question inevitably arises as to the depth of the agency representatives' new understanding of community representatives. To what extent does it represent real empathy rather than superficial accommodation to social changes over which they have no control? Are the agency representatives merely mouthing the proper words? One indication is that some of the comments about community representatives were patronizing and contradictory. For example, the comment "You have to involve people from the community" was followed by the statement "As long as you are opening up jobs what difference does it make if they are participating?" Another indication is that the agency representatives did not suggest that board membership changed their own roles within their agencies. They did not talk as if they had become more dedicated to working for change in their agencies.[39] But a counterindication is that several agency representatives expressed deep frustration at the unresponsiveness of their agencies to the problems of poverty people. This would suggest that their commitment was not merely superficial. A firmer assessment of the significance of agency representatives' socialization calls for study of the permanence of these changes and their impact on the representatives' behavior in their agencies.

The present data do not suggest any clear explanation of the patterns of socialization. Attempts to relate changes to the liberalism or conservatism of the members were not successful. The representatives from each agency, however, never reported similar changes in their general attitudes. Likewise, on certain issues representatives from the same agency were split in their attitudes. Thus one can speculate that on these issues prior personal socialization is a more important determinant of attitudinal change than is organizational position or role. But these issues were not directly related to EYOA; they were attitudes toward federalism, militancy, and liberalism. In contrast, representatives from the same agency exhibited marked similarity of attitudes toward EYOA, the staff, and the community representatives.[40] Here it is possible to describe the typical attitudes of the educators, the politicians, and the bureaucrats. Even though representatives from any one of these groups may differ in their general attitudes on militancy, for example, their attitudes toward EYOA are in general agreement. The best example of agency solidarity is the one agency's delegation that was uniformly negative on all three EYOA-related issues. On these issues organizational position or role seemed to be a more important determinant of attitudes than on the other issues. There was an agency position on them. While this might be expected in regard to EYOA and its staff, it is interesting that it also holds true for receptivity toward community representatives.

In summary, the evidence on the socialization of the agency representatives supports the generalization that adult socialization will concern concrete orientations rather than fundamental political loyalties.[41] The agency representatives changed the least in their ideological positions (that is, their identification as liberals or conservatives and their attitudes toward militancy), but on specific issues closely linked to information obtained from EYOA membership they changed more noticeably (attitudes toward community representatives and the federal government). Turning to the socialization of community representatives, we shall find evidence of more resocialization taking place, greater changes, and changes of a more fundamental nature.

CHANGES IN THE ATTITUDES OF THE ORIGINAL
COMMUNITY REPRESENTATIVES

While the agency representatives tended to de-emphasize the importance of their own changes in attitude, many of them expressed interest in finding out more about how the community representatives' attitudes had changed. Twelve agency representatives indicated that they had seen marked positive changes in the community representatives.[42]

The positive change they described most often was a lessening of hostility toward the agency representatives as the community representatives became more a part of the board and found that the agency representatives would not bite. One explained that the community people discovered that there are two sides to the coin and "the establishment is not so bad, fairly decent people as a whole." One agency representative illustrated the increased sense of responsibility by noting that one community representative said to a newly elected community representative "now that you are on the board you can't make damned fool statements anymore." The agency representatives indicated that the lessening of hostility toward the agency representatives carried over into a less hostile attitude toward the war on poverty and toward the agencies' programs. The program mentioned most was the school program.

Another category of change in community representatives described by the agency representatives was increase in understanding of what was going on in the board meetings and realism about the limitations placed on EYOA. Agency representatives also talked about the community representatives' personal growth, namely the development of self-confidence, a sense of security in working with others, and a willingness to discuss positions and listen to the other side.

When one turns to see how the community representatives felt they had changed, there are some interesting comparisons between community representatives' and agency representatives' perceptions of community representatives' changes. Further, there are interesting comparisons between the agency representatives' descriptions of their own changes and community representatives' perceptions of their own changes.

First, most of the community representatives agreed with the agency representatives that they had changed quite noticeably during their membership on the board. Six of the community representatives answered the question about changes in themselves with no hesitation or disclaimers, and only two denied changing. Table 17 compares the

TABLE 17

Board Members' Perceptions of Whether They Had Changed

Perception	Old community representatives		Agency representatives	
	Number	Percent	Number	Percent
Change	6	75	12	71
No change	2	25	5	24

responses to questions about changes in themselves made by the agency representatives and by the community representatives. Although the percentages of those who said they had changed in both groups are similar, the impression from the interviews was that the community representatives who are categorized here as "yes" did not add the same number of disclaimers that the agency representatives who said "yes" did. This may be interpreted either as greater frankness or willingness to be introspective or as an actual difference in the amount or significance of the learning that went on. The latter interpretation was made by the agency representatives and the staff members who have worked closely with the board. They feel that the agency people have changed less than the community people. The explanation is that the experience is not as novel for the agency members and they know what their agencies will permit since the agencies are well structured.

A second comparison between the community representatives and agency representatives' perceptions of how the community representatives had changed is that the community representatives did not indicate that their changes were all positive. Yet they did talk freely of many positive changes and these will be discussed first.

Many of the community representatives did mention the positive changes in understanding and personal growth which the agency representatives had perceived in them.[43] They described very movingly their feelings during the first months of being on the board. One said, "In the beginning I was terrified to tell the truth; not used to all the pressures; didn't know a soul and had never even been downtown before; I think the first year all of us were confused." Another said, "I was in tears several times as I left meetings because it was all so frustrating and I was really upset, budget and things, and I didn't know the first thing about how to read them." One representative explained that he did not know the terms used and that the other board members were "talking figures which don't mean anything to you at all. Here I am living off $120 a month, 16 million dollars and I don't even know what they are talking about. I don't know if it's a good salary or nothing. You don't know if it's right or too much—how much does a consultant cost? I never had a consultant. My minister was my consultant."

But all these representatives went on to say that they felt they had learned how the board worked and "what to look for in proposals and all that." They said that originally they had tried to reach for the moon but they found things just don't happen that way and gradually gained an understanding of the way things work. They indicated that they had learned how to talk to agency representatives before meetings and at breaks to explain their points of view. And they had found there are ways to change things that they were told could not be changed. One said: "A lot of things they said aren't possible are possible." Another explained that even if the Office of Economic Opportunity says things are a certain way, there are ways of changing them if you want to.[44]

Five of the community representatives also gave examples of personal growth. One explained that he had gained more experience and confidence in talking with the big people. He said, "I thought I had a little wall in between me so that I couldn't express myself, but then I came up to your height to learn how to talk with this kind of man." Another indicated growth of confidence by saying: "At times I felt I wasn't that important; I was learning, yes, sitting side by side with professional people, but I wasn't contributing anything. But now I feel I did have a little something to do somewhere along the line." Still another said: "I don't worry about myself and the kids as much as I used to, what's going to happen if I die. I think that's because I think they are proud that I'm doing what I'm doing." Another said that the experience had helped him learn to calm down and not take things too personally.

Comparing their responses about changes in themselves with those of the agency representatives shown in table 18, the total num-

TABLE 18

Comparison of Types of Changes in Board Members

Type of change	Agency representatives	Community representatives
Increase in understanding of how board operated	4	6
Increase in personal confidence and skills	3	5
Increase in hostility to EYOA	1	5
Increase in understanding of other group	11	4
Total mentions of change	19	20

ber of changes mentioned by agency representatives is less than that mentioned by community representatives. This supports the conclusion that the agency representatives changed less than the community representatives. Table 18 also shows that agency representatives talked about increases in confidence and understanding less often than the community representatives. The interpretation of this difference can go in two directions. It may indicate an absence of frankness or self-awareness in the agency representatives or an actual difference in the confidence and knowledge that the two groups bring to the board. Accepting the latter interpretation, the differences are indicative of the feelings of status differential that are at work—one group feeling informed and confident and the other group lacking confidence and information.

Perhaps the most interesting aspect of the community representatives' comments on their own changes, however, was that their attitudes toward the agency representatives, and especially the war on poverty and the agency's programs, had not become nearly as positive as the agency representatives had thought.[45] This difference is shown in table 19. The findings do not support the expectation that the community representatives will change so much that they will be indistinguishable from the agency representatives. In other words, the

community representatives did not become establishment-oriented or
downtown-oriented.[46]

Four of the community representatives did speak of some increase in understanding of the agency representatives. One subject
said he had to conclude they were sincere even though he had heard

TABLE 19

Comparison of Agency Representatives' and
Community Representatives' Perception of Types
of Changes in Community Representatives

Type of change	Agency representatives	Community representatives
Increase in understanding of how the board operates	7	6
Increase in personal confidence and skills	7	5
Increase in hostility toward EYOA	0	5
Increase in understanding of agency representatives	9	4

negative things about the establishment. Another said, "I became a
little more compassionate, rather than believing that they were going
to do wrong from the beginning like I did at first." But then he added
that "I haven't completely gotten out of that, but I do think we
changed some of their minds and they changed my mind over a period
of time." But all the representatives also made statements which indicated a sense of continuing distance from the agency representatives,
a continuing sense of we and they.[47]

The carry-over of the positive feelings about agency representatives to the war on poverty was not nearly as great as the agency representatives had indicated. Five of the community representatives
indicated an increased hostility toward the war on poverty and
EYOA. One said he had gotten more understanding of dirty politics
and more disgusted. Another said he had gotten more insight into
what he described as the "dirty lowdown unrealistic things they do in
politics and lawmaking." In these cases an increase in understanding
was accompanied by a negative affective reaction.

Note that while only one agency representative out of sixteen
stated that his attitudes toward EYOA had become more negative
after being on the board, five out of eight community representatives
talked that way (see table 18). Thus while the preponderant change

mentioned by agency representatives was increased tolerance of the community representatives, the reverse was not true. A majority of the community representatives did not mention increased trust of agency representatives, and the ones who did saw it as a mutual process. And while one agency representative became more hostile to the program many more community representatives did.[48] An increased understanding of how things worked and a gain in personal confidence was not necessarily linked with an increase in positive attitudes toward the program. Similarly, an increase in trust of agency people was not necessarily linked with an increase in positive attitude toward the program.

The community representatives' changes in attitudes show that any attempt to label community representatives as cop-outs or to equate participation or increase in information with positive evaluation is much too crude. If the agency representatives think that having community representatives on CAAs will make them into supporters of community action agencies, they will be very disappointed with these findings. If, on the other hand, they want to increase the representatives' feelings of personal effectiveness and their understanding, the results here suggest that membership on the board is conducive to these ends. Judging from the functioning of the board, their personal changes do not have an impact on the board's power balance, but they may have an effect on the attitudes of the future activities in the community and thus indirectly on the poverty community that the community representatives come into contact with.

Just as the agency representatives were asked about certain changes which they did not volunteer themselves, community representatives were asked specifically about changes in their attitudes toward various agencies, individual efficacy, federal involvement in the poverty program, militancy, and liberalism and conservatism. Again the findings are not very clear except in the first two areas, but they do give a fuller picture of the thinking of the community representatives (table 20). Attempts were also made to find out how their participation in politics and voluntary organizations and their life situations has changed as a result of involvement in EYOA. The picture here is much clearer.

The changes in attitudes toward specific agencies which seemed most marked were, as the agency representatives correctly perceived, toward the schools. Six out of seven responses indicated a change in the direction of feeling more positive toward the schools. One said that he had felt that the "people way up there do not know the problems of the people way down here" but he talked with the school men and found they were aware, they were okay.

The answers to questions about changes in attitude toward the

TABLE 20

Attitudes of the Original Community Representatives after Being on the Board

Attitudes toward	Positive	Negative	No answer
Agency representatives	5	3	0
EYOA	3	5	0
Staff	4	3	1
Schools	6	1	1
City	0	7	1
Political efficacy	7	0	1
Militancy	3+4	0	1
Democrat self-image	7	1	0

city were mixed. Only one community representative clearly indicated a less hostile attitude toward the city. He said that he still does not agree with Mayor Yorty but that he now sees that his extremely bad original opinion of him was a little unfair. Two other community representatives indicated that their original negative opinion of city government became more negative after being on EYOA because they felt the mayor was trying to control it. The three other community representatives who responded indicated that their opinions were negative but that they had not changed one way or the other.[49] One suspects that the community representatives would change their opinion of the city government if its leadership changed. Their comments show that they are not the deeply alienated and bitter types who would respond negatively to any mention of government.[50]

The scale of political efficacy used in the social sciences[51] was of interest in designing this research, and the hope was to be able to measure the feelings of efficacy of both the agency representatives and the community representatives. But the indexes used for large samples were obviously not applicable to subjects with this degree of sophistication in an open-ended interview situation. So the decision was simply to use a general question, "How much influence do you think an ordinary individual can have on government?"[52]

The results with community representatives were not as revealing as their comments on the poverty program, the agency representatives, and their personal growth. Two community representatives said that an individual's influence depends on knowing the right people and channels and they both said they feel they can have more influence after being on the board. One representative said he always felt individuals could have some influence, especially if they unite. Four other representatives indicated they felt able to influence government. They stressed their ability to talk with government officials or to initiate boycotts and riots if certain actions were not taken. Accordingly, at least five of the community representatives had a high sense of efficacy before being on the board and the board did not decrease it; the board increased it in at least two cases.

Social science tends to equate efficacy with an absence of hostility, and in the community representatives' cases this clearly does not apply. The community representatives are characterized both by efficacy and hostility toward EYOA. Their disappointment with EYOA did not lead to decline in efficacy; instead there was a slight increase. This pattern suggests the limitation of the concept of efficacy as developed in the literature. It is linked to a middle-class League of Women Voters' notion of citizenship. The pattern of efficacy and affect among some revolutionaries might parallel that of the community representatives, hostility plus efficacy. Social science literature suggests that people feel more positive toward the local rather than the national government. This certainly held true with the agency representatives.[53] But the community representatives did not differentiate between their attitudes toward local and federal government. Both levels were lumped together as part of the "they."

The responses on militancy, like the responses about EYOA, do not suggest a predominance or an increase of downtown orientation among the community representatives. None of the community representatives indicated that their attitudes toward militancy had changed because of their being on the board, though they were not hesitant to admit other changes. Three of the community representatives indicated they were very militant. Sears found 22 to 30 percent of curfew area residents favored the black nationalist groups.[54] The percentage of community representatives favoring such groups is similar, so on this basis the community representatives would not be deviant poor. They stated support for the Brown Berets, boycotts, sit-ins, and Malcolm X. None openly advocated violence, and stressed instead legal means of "raising hell" to change the system in a constructive manner, but they were sympathetic to violence in certain interactions where other methods had not worked. One explained, "I wouldn't go out and start a fight but I'd help one along, I really would." The other community representatives expressed more qualified militancy; they expressed more trust and more reluctance to use violence. But they were not opposed to militancy the way the agency representatives generally were. All of them stressed the need to be aggressive, to use militancy through normal channels, to unite in pushing for what they want.[55] They said they were supporters of Martin Luther King and Cesar Chavez but that if Ries Tijerina and Rap Brown get things done in their way that is fine too. The preponderance of positive response to militancy among community representatives contrasts with the negative reactions among agency representatives. The community representatives' responses on militancy suggest that five of them could be classified as moderates and three as militants or at least as more militant than the others.[56]

The political party identification of the community representatives included six registered Democrats, one registered Republican, and one who declined to register in either party.[57] This pattern paralleled recollections of parental party loyalties except in three cases where members said that so far as they knew their parents did not have a party identification or never voted. Only two said they were liberal Democrats, one adding that he was radical. None mentioned any change in party identification or liberalness owing to their experience on the board.

Social scientists' studies of participation stress a correlation between low income and low participation in organizations and politics. The interviews with community representatives revealed clear examples of changes in their participation patterns after they became members of the EYOA board.[58] As shown in table 21, the community representatives deviate from the typical low income group pattern because they all say they had voted prior to EYOA and three had worked in campaigns. Further, all except two were involved in at least one organization before joining EYOA. Only two mentioned holding offices in the organizations or doing anything more than going to meetings (and one of these was motivated by the war on poverty to become active in a political organization). Thus the picture that emerges is not of isolates, but neither is it one of experienced organizational members with many links in the community. Only two of the community representatives would fit the latter description.

Seven of the community representatives stressed the impact that being on the board had on their interest in politics and on their organizational involvement.[59] They said they were much more involved

TABLE 21

Changes in the Participation of the
Original Community Representatives

	Before	After
Voting	8	8
Work in campaigns	3	3
Belong to 0 organizations	2	1
Belong to 1 organization	1	0
Belong to 2 organizations	5	1
Belong to 3 or more organizations	0	6
Responsible position in organizations	2	6

now and listed numerous organizational memberships. The community representatives who had not formerly been very active were activated by board membership; as one said, "Now I'm involved up to my ears." The two who had been highly involved before said they had become even more involved.

This finding suggests that community action programs, even when their purpose is not primarily one of organizing the poor, do have the effect of increasing the community activity of the poor who serve on the board.[60] The increases in the community representatives' feelings of effectiveness and in their information may be linked with increased participation in community activities. Thus membership on the EYOA board may have significance not just for the individuals' attitudes but also for the community in which the individuals become more active participants and leaders.

The community representatives' comments about changes in their life situation were not nearly so positive. Half of them stressed that they were worse off financially after being on the board than they had been before. They stressed that the payment of $25 per day of board business was not enough to support their families and yet the time commitments required by the board prevented them from holding regular jobs which would support their families. Several indicated they had been forced to quit previous jobs in order to fulfill their board obligations.

These comments were made by the representatives soon after they left the board. A check on the jobs the representatives took after leaving the board suggests that although their financial situation may have deteriorated while they were on the board, it may improve after leaving the board. Two of them were hired in poverty programs. Two applied to poverty programs and were still hoping to get jobs. Another had not applied but hoped to get a job in poverty-related programs when his family situation permitted. The indication is that board membership shapes the aspirations of board members toward jobs in poverty programs and that these aspirations are at least partially realized.[61] Board membership appears to be a transitional step toward private upward mobility for the community representatives.

The fact that community representatives move on to jobs in poverty programs leads to criticism from certain community and professional people. They resent the new careers and point to them as proof that the community representatives lose an interest in poor people and become oriented to downtown. A more accurate analysis seems to be that the community representatives try not to lose contact with the poor because their career possibilities depend on their ability to provide links to the indigenous community. What we have is the emergence of a new role, the professional poor person, which parallels the civil rights leaders who become professional blacks.[62] Private upward mobility does not mean that the community representatives sell out. It merely means that their own economic position improves while their orientation remains distinct from the agency members of the board.

A review of changes in the community representatives shows marked increases in knowledge and personal confidence (see table 22) and at the same time increases in hostility toward the war on poverty and the city. On the whole, however, they showed an increase in trust of individual agency representatives and of the school programs. There were indications of increases in feelings of efficacy, but no perceptible changes in feelings about the local and national government, and no decline in militancy. There were also marked increases in participation in community organizations. The conclusion is that participation on the EYOA board did not make major shifts in the affective orientation of the community representatives. They still maintained a local orientation as opposed to a downtown orientation. But there were major changes in their feelings about their own ability to get things done, in their participation patterns, and later in their economic positions.

This socialization of the community representatives challenges the proposition that basic political attitudes are not changed in adults. EYOA appears to be a stimulus for many changes, and changes of a

TABLE 22

Changes in the Original Community Representatives

Attitudes toward	Number of changes in positive direction	Number of changes in negative direction
Increase in understanding of how the board operates	6	0
Increase in personal confidence and skills	5	0
Increase in hostility to EYOA	5	1
Increase in trust of agency representatives	4	0
Increase in participation	6	0
Schools	6	0
City	1	2
Political efficacy	2	0
Federal government	0	0
Militancy	0	0
Democrat self-image	0	0
Republican self-image	0	0

fundamental type in the community representatives. It is true that like the agency representatives, the community representatives do not change their ideological position, but the increases in personal confidence and participation are important changes in political attitudes. This socialization appears to mark the abandonment of childhood patterns and a fundamental change in the political attitudes of these adults.[63]

The significance of this pattern depends partly upon how long it persists. A follow-up study of these community representatives is needed to see how these attitudes and behavior are modified as time passes. How long do the changed attitudes continue? It is possible that board membership will contribute indirectly to the development of a downtown orientation by giving the representatives the experience that will qualify them for stable jobs that will decrease their hostility and lead them to identify with downtown. But as suggested above, their career possibilities as professional poor depend on their maintaining a certain hostility to downtown. So even if they mellow internally they may have to maintain outwardly hostile attitudes. Downtown does not reward them for talking downtown; the reward comes for professional poor who talk militant language while still being willing to compromise. The data on changes in community representatives do not suggest any clear explanation of why the different representatives changed in specific ways. This problem is discussed in the following chapter on changes in the new community representatives.

In conclusion, this examination of the effect of board membership on the board members suggests that the experience has had an impact on the socialization of both agency and community representatives. But the community people change more fundamentally than the agency people. The community representatives have influenced the attitudes of agency representatives in the direction of more toleration of participation by the poor. On the other hand, contact with agency representatives has made a marked increase in the knowledge, confidence, and participation of the community representatives.

These changes do not negate the problem of co-optation discussed in the preceding chapter. Nevertheless, it seems important to be aware of the changes in socialization that are occurring in the Los Angeles community action program and may well be occurring in many other community action programs throughout the nation. These individual changes can provide support for larger changes in society. If further analysis of the persistence and depth of the changes confirms these findings, it would seem important that the participation of the poor on boards not be rejected unless the alternative enables such changes in socialization to continue. Brim points out that when attempts to resocialize an individual to accept the status quo are ineffective, one possible result is that the expectations of those in the establishment will be changed to accord with the formerly deviant actor's performance or objectives.[64] To the extent that the community representatives maintain their own perspectives while at the same time gaining skills and confidence in communicating more effectively with agency representatives, it is possible that they can serve as sources of change in the agency representatives and in local communities even though they do not actually gain power over the immediate decisions made by the board.

6. The Board's Effect on the Attitudes of the New Community Representatives

During the course of this project the election of new community representatives provided a chance to avoid reliance on retrospective recall. The seven new community representatives (one incumbent was reelected) were interviewed before they met with the board,[1] were observed on the board for six months, and then were reinterviewed. The results seem worthy of consideration in a separate chapter, as a case study within a case study, because they illuminate what "maximum feasible participation" means in individual terms. The results also provide a valuable check on the retrospective recall data on the original community representatives described in the preceding chapter. The existence of the two types of data on poverty people makes it possible to draw firmer conclusions about the effect of board membership on community representatives.

The recruitment and campaigning of the new community representatives were described in chapter 3. The same section compares their socioeconomic characteristics with those of the original representatives. In general the new representatives were more involved in poverty-related organizations than the original representatives (though not in other organizations before the war on poverty started), were younger, and included no Negro males and one additional Caucasion. They also had lived in Los Angeles longer, had less education and fewer children. Their activity in community organizations had made a greater jump above their parents' activity than the activity of the original community representatives had in comparison with their parents. The reverse was true of political activity—the original community representatives had made a greater jump above their parents' political interests than the new community representatives had.

This chapter first describes the community representatives as they were before they joined the board, their attitudes toward EYOA and politics, and their expectations about membership on the EYOA board. Then there is a discussion of how the community representatives changed after six months on the board based on their own comments in the reinterview and the observations of the author. These changes are compared with the changes in the original community representatives. Then their observations about board membership are presented and their social mobility is considered. The chapter closes with some generalizations about changes in community representatives based on the two sets of representatives.

ATTITUDES BEFORE

The initial interviews revealed that the community representatives had very little information about the Economic and Youth Opportunities Agency or the board to which they had just been elected.[2] Most gave only vague answers to a question about the purpose of EYOA. A typical response was: "I really can't answer that because I don't know much. I haven't studied it carefully; I'll have to find out about it first." Only one representative had ever been to a board meeting. One indicated that he had not known until recently that board meetings were open, so he had never attended. They did not distinguish between the EYOA staff, delegate agency staffs, and the board. None could answer a question about which groups were getting the most from EYOA or had the most influence on the board.

Like the original representatives, several of the new representatives expressed nervousness about the impending experience. One explained that when EYOA called and said he had won he felt: "complete panic . . . oh my God, now what do I do? Now I really have to do something. Before it was all talk and now I have to get out and do it." Others exhibited confidence during the interview and talked of specific projects they wanted to get started. Later, however, these too talked of fears; one explained "we didn't have education enough to speak up, didn't know how to go about it, didn't know Robert's Rules or anything else."

The community representatives were evenly split in their attitudes toward EYOA. Three chose to stress the positive accomplishments of EYOA. They mentioned areas for improvement such as job training but indicated that the problems were not EYOA's fault. They said more money was needed but that was not possible because of the Vietnam war. Three community representatives expressed hostile feelings toward EYOA, blaming it for the failures in the war on poverty.[3] One blamed the failures on board members not really listening: "While they are there at the board meetings, oh yes, they are all fired up to do something, but when they leave, maybe one out of all of them are going to do something, but the rest aren't. If they are going to get those pay checks, well then, earn it." They said that owing to such failures EYOA was losing the faith of the people.

None of the community representatives knew any of the agency representatives on the board, but their descriptions of EYOA showed their distrust of the agency representatives. Two community representatives were exceptions. One said the people on the board were sincerely interested in poverty, nice people trying to work things out. The other said that he thought the agency representatives would be able to tell who was sincere and would cooperate at times because "they got feelings you know but it just got to be aroused."

The community representatives were split in their attitudes toward public and private agencies. Three representatives made very negative comments about the schools. They said the schools "stink," "doin' nothin'." One explained: "They are not really concerned with Head Start. They cooperate with the playgrounds but as far as Head Start they never send notices home to the mothers. They are concerned with why the Head Start child is doing something they can't get their kindergarten child to do. They ought to get on the ball with their children; do you know what I mean? They are concerned with the Board of Education and that's that!" Four were not negative toward the schools but said there is room for improvement.

Three of the four representatives who commented on the city government expressed hostility toward it.[4] They said that "the city fathers don't know what life is like down here"; "they just sit up there and judge." One explained: "Once you're educated you don't come down to the level of the poor people." They had complaints about lighting, streets, and garbage. The only person who mentioned the police said he was not as critical of them as he was of other city activities because the police are needed even though they do make mistakes. One said that Mayor Yorty was "serving about like Lurleen Wallace."

The question about county government was clarified by mentioning welfare because the respondents were vague about what county government was. Four were critical of welfare. Two of these cited bad social workers who threaten the recipients and don't show them how the process works. The two positive comments came from representatives who said they had had no contact with welfare but thought things were getting better. One of these said taxpayers are the only ones who might complain about county programs; "when you look at your taxes, you know how well they [the county] been servin' you." Three community representatives were very critical of voluntary agencies, and two of these specifically criticized the hypocrisy of the church on the race and poverty issue. One explained: "You know why I don't go to church? Tired of a fashion show and tired of someone telling me I'm a sinner living in hell when there isn't anyone trying to help me change the way I'm living." Three community representatives praised the work done by private agencies.

The responses to questions concerning political efficacy illustrate a wide range of reactions and suggest some of the difficulties in the index ordinarily used. When the community representatives were asked how much influence an ordinary individual can have on government, three gave what would traditionally be classified as efficacious responses. They said that people can change governments, that one vote can make a lot of difference, and that people can have a lot of influence if they get together with other people. One of these added that before the riots he had not known that ordinary people could have as much influence as the rioters had. Two other community representatives indicated that some ordinary individuals can have influence but they implied that they themselves did not. One of these explained that to have influence you have to have a "little bit of education, to know how to express yourself. If you don't they'll laugh at you." He cited examples where he had been laughed at. The other two community representatives gave typical nonefficacious answers, saying that ordinary individuals do not have much influence.

Thus the community representatives might seem to be about evenly divided among those who feel politically efficacious and those who do not. But the community representatives' answers to a second question often used as an index of efficacy make them all appear to be low in political efficacy. Six out of the seven community representatives felt that public officials do not listen to ordinary individuals.

The community representatives indicated that public officials listen only if they have to. For example, one said: "it takes a lot of talkin' and a lot of people before you can get them to listen. If I walk up to a politician and start talkin' it don't mean a thing to him." Another told the story of a city official who was angry when the radio said children in his area did not have milk: "He doesn't realize that maybe it could be true; he's always had it, milk for his children and himself. Once you're educated you don't come down to the level of the poor people." He added that individuals will not be listened to alone, so they have to stand together in a group. Thus, on the standard index of political efficacy the representatives would have low scores.[5]

But the conclusion drawn here from a combination of the responses to the two questions is that the community representatives have a realistic awareness of the difficulties of being listened to, and about half of them feel able to have some influence through group activities even though they have doubts about their ability as leaders of groups. The contrasting conclusions that can be reached about their responses underline the need to rework the index of efficacy so that finer distinctions can be made between types of responses. For example, in some settings the answer that government officials do not listen would be given by those with a realistic picture of government as well as those who are bitterly alienated from government. Similarly the index should be designed to distinguish between the different reasons people have for saying that individuals do not have influence. Attempts were made to determine the community representatives' attitudes toward the federal government as opposed to local and state government. But they did not have very definite impressions and the results were inconclusive.

Only two of the community representatives indicated they were very militant. They said that the one who gets the most is "the one who was the loudest, fights the hardest." One explained: "Don't give up, if you really want something. Give your local officials a chance, present it to them and tell them what you want, but if that doesn't work go to a little higher, and then if that doesn't work do what you got to do. Take whatever steps you've got to take." These representatives identified with Tijerina and one described himself as a very violent person, but the example of violence given was "I yell when I have to yell." Thus while these two representatives thought of themselves as militant, they did not openly advocate violence but instead expressed sympathy with those who do. The five other community representatives could be classified as moderates. They were critical of Tijerina, Malcolm X, and the Brown Berets. Instead they expressed approval for King and Chavez. Yet they urged the need to get angry and fight for changes in nonviolent ways, including marches and boycotts. One explained there are reasons why people are violent and "we must find out those reasons and do something about them if we are going to prevent it in the future."

All seven of the community representatives indicated that they were registered Democrats and six of them said both their parents had been Democrats (the one exception said his parents were not registered). Only one community representative qualified his party identification by referring to the type of Democrat he was; he said he was middle-of-the-road. The terms "liberal" or "conservative" did not have meaning to most of them.[6]

The organizational and political participation of the community representatives was described in chapter 3. The community representatives were typically involved in three or more organizations. But prior to the war on poverty, only two had belonged to organizations. They also described themselves, with one exception, as voters interested in politics. Some of their comments on political campaigns, however, indicated a very low level of information. For example, one of the representatives who said he was very interested in politics responded to a question about whether he voted for Brown or Nixon in 1962 by saying, "Nixon never ran for governor in this state."

A review of the responses given in the first interviews leads to the conclusion that the community representatives did not fit into either the allegiant or alienated categories.[7] Like the first set of community representatives, the new ones were not deeply estranged from government. They had not rejected government, as is shown by their voting and their participation in war on poverty organizations. But they certainly are not allegiants in the same way as Lane's subjects. The community representatives are supporters of the political order but they are critical of many of the institutions in that order.[8] They are angrier about their place in the social system than Lane's men and less hopeful about their ability to improve the situation.[9] The sense of satisfaction or at least resignation that Lane's men expressed was not characteristic of the community representatives. They are best described as militantly allegiant or moderately alienated. Prior to joining the

board, elected representatives in Los Angeles would be located somewhere in the middle area of the continuum between alienated and
allegiant.

Before going on to discuss the community representatives' expectations about EYOA, an attempt must be made to explain the
participation of the community representatives in the war on poverty.
Almond and Verba[10] suggest that participation in families, schools,
and jobs facilitates participation in politics and organization. While
their explanation may apply to survey data, it does not help explain
the participation of the community representatives in poverty organizations. None of them felt they had had influence on their family decisions and only three had stable families in which participation
would have been possible. The other four described difficult family
situations, such as the early death of both parents which forced the
child to raise himself or hostility between a step-parent and child, or
hostility between parents which resulted in the child feeling rejected.

Almond and Verba say participatory experience in school or on
the job can compensate for lack of participation in the family. But
four of the community representatives did not find school congenial
and did not participate in class or extracurricular activities. Three of
them quit before finishing high school. One said: "I didn't care about
Lincoln or when he died or his family or nothing; I wanted to learn
something to go out and use, make a living. I should have cared
about English but it wasn't tied in." Only three indicated participation in organizations while in school.[11] And the career patterns of
the representatives indicate that participation would not be very likely
(see chapter 3). Prior to their participation in the war on poverty
activities, six had participated in one or fewer organizations and four
of the community representatives had not participated in organizations at all. They said they were too busy working or that the
organizations were too boring.

What then explains why these people get involved in the war on
poverty? If prior participation in family, school, and jobs do not
account for it, what does? As suggested in chapter 3, the answer
seems to lie partly in the convergence of personal invitations to join
or close proximity to an organization, with personal circumstances
which made joining possible and more desirable than it had been in
the past. For example, most were dissatisfied with their personal
lives or their jobs and were looking for something that would increase

their satisfaction. The switch from withdrawal to participation was not linked with either positive or negative attitudes toward the political system. The other part of the answer may relate to personal efficacy. Almost all the community representatives mentioned being either outspoken or hardworking. They talked about not giving up no matter what happens. They did not talk as if they were defeated; they talked as if they felt in control of themselves. They expressed a sense of ego strength. Hostility, yes, as shown in their attitudes toward officials, but lack of personal efficacy, no.[12]

One wonders where the sense of efficacy comes from. The most noticeable common aspect in the past of all the community representatives is the presence of one parent they identify with. The three representatives from stable famlies expressed admiration for one or both of their parents. But it was noticeable that two of those from unstable families or families in which participation was not allowed, spoke in terms that showed they identified with one of their parents and saw their own participation as adults as similar to that parent's own participation. These parents were models for them. Two, however, did not talk this way. One seemed to have gained a feeling of confidence from having worked hard all his life and succeeded by his own efforts in establishing a stable life. People had always told him that he was special, that he had the "mind of a rich kid," that he would make good, and he tried to live up to it. The second is hardest to explain; he had no model and felt no one had ever been for him. He stressed a turning point in his life which made him "wake up" and see that he was heading in the same wrong direction that his parents had gone.

The life histories of the new community representatives point up the need to revise the social science explanations of participation in order to account more adequately for the fact that low income people do become participants in organization even though they have had little prior experience as participants. We now move on to consider the community representatives' expectations about membership on the EYOA board.

EXPECTATIONS ABOUT BOARD MEMBERSHIP

All the community representatives said in the first interview that they would be representing the interests of poor people. Four of them specifically said they would be representing impoverished people in their own districts. The other three community representatives said they would have to consider not just their own districts but poor people in all districts. None of the representatives indicated that they would represent a specific organization or work through one organization.

In response to a question about how they planned to find out what their constituents wanted, they all mentioned going to various community meetings and calling special community meetings. Only two of the representatives said that it would be impossible to represent such large districts. They were critical of EYOA for setting up districts where a person from Venice is supposed to represent Pacoima twenty miles away, or a person from Pomona is supposed to represent San Fernando and Lancaster, more than thirty miles from Pomona. One representative said: "EYOA is telling the representatives that they have to cover this territory and all these people. . . . I'm sorry, but it can't be done." Only two community representatives were critical of EYOA for not providing the representatives with more assistance in their jobs. During the first months of their term, however, several more became very critical. They mentioned that the $25 per day of board business did not cover expenses, and asked for offices in the community for meetings or at least an answering service and secretarial help. They pointed out that the agency representatives had these conveniences but the community representatives did not.

The community representatives had little knowledge about the original community representatives or the other newly elected ones. They had not contacted the original community representative from their districts for advice. They seemed to be isolated individuals chosen by their own subcommunities, to face alone an experience about which they knew very little. Whereas the original community representatives expressed marked distrust of the other community representatives, the newly elected community representatives did not. They were interested in finding out what the other new representatives were like,[13] and stressed the importance of working closely with them. They talked of joining forces and helping each other. One said, "I'm going to offer them, you help me and I'll help you."

Five of the community representatives used words like "fighter," "aggressive," and "outspoken" to describe what kind of board member they would be. They said that the one who fights the hardest gets the programs. One of them said, "Once I feel obligated I give it all I've got and I always feel like I must win. . . . I don't even let my personal life interfere with my obligation to the community." The other two community representatives said that they would try to work things out congenially rather than with a blast.

All the community representatives were asked to speculate on the effect the board might have on them and their community's opinion of them. Two were puzzled by the question and said that they did not see how the board could affect them. One pointed out that people might blame him if he failed to help them with their problems even if the problems were things he could not do anything about, but that people would also give him credit if the problems got solved whether or not he was the one responsible. The four other community representatives said that being on the board would test what kind of people they really were. They said that they expected people on the board are "kind of beat down by the board; there is so much arguin' going on." They said the test was whether you give up or fight. One explained: "I'm going to find out just what kind of person I am; how far will I go to defend what I say and the people I say I want to help?" All indicated that they would not give up. One said he did not think "brown-nosing with big people" would change him because he's lived on "the other side before so it's no big deal" to him. Another said: "People are saying to me don't let them push you around. And I say maybe they can push me around and maybe they can't. We'll soon find out about that." They acknowledged that people in their communities expected them to perform miracles, "clean up the wine alleys and ghettos." They said they had been trying to convince their constituents that on many issues not within EYOA jurisdiction all they could do was refer them to the proper agency and that even on EYOA issues they could not accomplish anything without community backing.

The community representatives' expectations about the functioning of the board indicated they were frightened but optimistic, anxious to organize yet noticeably uninformed and unrealistic about the pressures and conflicts they would be subjected to. They seemed extremely vulnerable (somewhat similar to college freshmen at orientation meetings) and one wondered who they would end up listening to, who would get their ears, and what directions they would go in.

CHANGES IN THE NEW COMMUNITY REPRESENTATIVES
AND COMPARISONS WITH THE ORIGINAL
COMMUNITY REPRESENTATIVES

Six months after being elected to the EYOA board the new community representatives all agreed they had changed because of their experiences on the board, and like the original community representatives they talked about these changes without hesitation. The most frequently mentioned change was an increase in understanding of how the board works. All seven of the new community representatives admitted that when they first joined the board they knew very little about it, and like the original community representatives they felt they had learned a lot about what was going on. This increase in information was confirmed when all seven were able to give direct answers to questions about the purpose of EYOA and to make distinctions between the staff and the board.[14] Most of the representatives also mentioned learning about strategies for influencing the board. For example, they mentioned learning techniques to win people to their side by manipulating and using psychology instead of just arguing; learning to let the agency representatives try to get thirteen yes votes rather than to try to get thirteen no votes themselves.

Four of the community representatives also talked about a growth in confidence. Several indicated that they liked having contact with a different circle of people than they had associated with before. One explained: "It feels pretty good to be mixing with these people there, well-educated you know. Thy have more experience. You learn something out of them." They said they had gained confidence in being able to get their points across to the board. One contrasted his current confidence with his previous situation this way: "I never finished high school, no association with politics, never worked in an office before, never had the challenge to sit with doctors and businessmen and to discuss and debate issues about other people's lives. . . . I never been in no board room or big meetings with big people and I figured it would scare me to death." The discovery that they could function in this setting left these four representatives with feelings of increased worth and satisfaction, the feeling that they are worthwhile, that they are "doing something."[15]

The interviews revealed, however, that in spite of general

changes in the direction of understanding and confidence, the community representatives were characterized by increased hostility toward EYOA. Four of the seven said they had become more disillusioned with EYOA.[16] They said their evaluations had "completely changed," that things were worse than they had expected, that they had lost their faith.

Their hostility was linked with their feelings that certain groups were running EYOA. Three said that they had discovered that the poor on the EYOA board were just being used.[17] The users were variously described as the staff, the established agencies, local, state, and national politicians, and the middle class. One community representative explained that "the community is just being used . . . they just do these things so the government will give them the money and that's it." Another commented: "If they really want something they will do it without us. They bring up a lot of things on that board. . . . They are just trying in a nice way to get a consent, but they are going to do it anyway."

When these representatives were asked to specify what groups really ran EYOA, they admitted that they were not sure but they knew there were such groups. One said, "From what I hear it is Washington, or San Francisco, big organizations, people who have power, like they say Hawkins, Cannon, or Opal Jones." Yet he indicated that he had learned that powerful people are not quite as powerful as he had thought. He said: "Before I didn't know so much that people could run other people. That people could put pressure on these people [leaders] and they would just fold, and bow their heads. . . . To me I thought that once you are up there you can do what you want, but its not. They are not big people. I feel sometimes bigger than they do." The quandary of the representatives who felt they were being used but were not sure by whom is strangely reminiscent of the plight of social scientists who attempt to grapple with the pluralist-elitist controversy—influence is real yet very elusive.

So far the changes in the new community representatives parallel the changes in the original community representatives: an increase in understanding and confidence is accompanied by a negative affective reaction toward EYOA, as shown in table 23. But what about the new representatives' attitudes toward the agency representatives? In March only two of the new community representatives made positive comments about agency representatives. Half a year later, six of the seven community representatives said they felt more positive toward the agency representatives. This appears to distinguish the new representatives from the original ones; only 50 percent of the original representatives said they felt more favorable to the agency repre-

TABLE 23

Comparison of Types of Changes Mentioned by
Original and New Community Representatives

Type of change	Original community representatives	New community representatives
Increase in understanding of how board operates	6	7
Increase in personal confidence and skills	5	4
Increase in hostility to EYOA	5	4
Increase in understanding of agency representatives	4	6

sentatives, while 85 percent of the new representatives did.[18] Yet the new representatives, like the earlier ones, indicated that they were ambivalent. A typical reply was that the agency representatives were more concerned than other people in their agencies, but that "they are not as concerned as they claim because they won't buck their own power structure, afraid of losing their jobs. They are talking but there is no action." During an interview a representative would refer to agency representatives first with trust, then with distrust; he would say "they're trying," and later say, "they don't care about the poor." Several mentioned incidents of personal contact with agency representatives in which they were surprised to find how much better agency people understood the poor than they had expected. They reacted favorably to agency people they felt took the time to talk frankly with representatives and who urged them to call when they had troubles, promising to try to see their side.[19]

The new community representatives reveal even more clearly than the old community representatives that positive feelings about agency representatives do not necessarily carry over to the war on poverty and EYOA. While six out of seven felt favorable toward the agency representative on the board, only three out of seven had a positive evaluation of EYOA. Study of the new community representatives also supports the generalization made in the preceding chapter that the most marked changes in community representatives are increases in understanding and feelings of personal effectiveness rather than in positive evaluations of community action agencies.

The new representatives were asked specifically about their attitudes toward various agencies, individual efficacy, the federal government, militancy, and party identification. The results are compared with those for the old community representatives in table 24.

TABLE 24

Comparison of the Changes in Original and New
Community Representatives on Specific Indicators

Type of change	Original community representatives	New community representatives
More positive toward schools	6	4
More positive toward city	1	0
Increase in efficacy	2	6
More positive to federal government	0	4
More militant	0	0
Democrat self-image	0	0
Republican self-image	0	1
Increase in participation	6	5

The comments by the new community representatives about various agencies are consistent with the pattern of remarks by the original representatives. In both groups attitudes toward the schools became more positive (table 24), but attitudes toward the city, county, and voluntary agencies did not show any clear trends. While some expressed positive feelings toward certain representatives from these agencies, these feelings were not consistently translated into positive feelings for the agencies. Nor did board membership significantly change their preexisting low levels of information about the city and county or their prior attitudes toward them and the voluntary agencies.

In contrast, the new community representatives showed very marked changes in their feelings of political efficacy. Six of the seven said individuals definitely could have more influence than they had thought before.[20] All six indicated they personally felt they had much more influence than before they were on the board, and most also talked much more confidently about the ability of people to influence government if they organize. Usually their assessments of whether or not they changed fit closely with the researcher's estimate, but here even more change was observed than they indicated. For example, one respondent implied that while his own sense of influence had definitely increased his opinion of the ordinary individual's influence had stayed about the same. Yet in the first interview when asked about the ordinary person's influence he merely said, "not very much. Public officials can have a lot of influence on the individual." In the second interview he repeated that the individual does not have very much but went on to speak with animation about the potential for influence. He said: "If the community gets together as a body they have something to say about government whether it is city, state, or federal. Now that people are having more to say about government, they don't like the kind of establishment we're under." Several respondents indicated similar increased stress on the importance of individuals working together to have influence.[21]

The responses to the second indicator of efficacy also show a change toward more efficacy, but not as many changed in this direction and the magnitude of the individual changes did not seem as great. As might be expected from the previously discussed increase in trust of agency representatives, four community representatives said that government officials listen more than they had thought previously. One mentioned his congressman calling him for advice. Yet they still added the stipulations given in the first interviews that officials listen only under certain conditions.[22]

In general, however, the new community representatives showed a marked increase in political efficacy. They felt that they themselves had more influence than before they were on the board. In the first interviews none of the representatives talked as if they were anything other than ordinary individuals. They did not see themselves as leaders. In the second interviews all of them talked about themselves as leaders, as distinct from the ordinary individuals implied in the question. This is an interesting change in self-image, a potentially significant increase in political efficacy. The significance will depend on whether the feelings continue after they leave the board.

Just as the new community representatives exhibited more increase in political efficacy than the original community representatives, they showed greater change in their attitudes toward the federal government. After six months on the board they had formed definite impressions about whether the federal or local government was more sympathetic to poor people. Four of them had become much more positive toward the national government, which meant that a total of six out of seven favored the federal level.[23] For example, one representative originally said that there is too much interference from the federal government, but in the second interview he said that the federal government has a more enlightened view of poverty than the state and local governments, and "our main hope lies in Washington."

The responses to questions about militancy did not show any clear changes. The same two community representatives identified themselves as militants, sympathetic to the Brown Berets and Tijerina. The five moderates continued to urge aggressive actions that stayed within the laws. Comparison with the original representatives shows that in both groups the more militant representatives were in the minority (three out of eight in the first, two out of seven in the second) and the division within the groups was quite similar. In addition, both the members who are here classified as militant were very moderate militants when compared with militants active in the poverty community. Yet the new community representatives, like the old, were significantly more sympathetic to militants than other members of the EYOA board and did not seem to become less militant owing to participation on the board. Only one representative indicated any change in feelings about political parties; he liked the national Republican candidate's stress on jobs instead of welfare.

The general pattern of responses on most of the items has been that changes are more apparent in the new representatives than in the old.[24] This is not true, however, when we consider the participation patterns of the new community representatives; they have not changed as greatly as the original representatives did. Five out of seven of the new community representatives said they were more active in the community than they were before EYOA. This division is similar to the six out of eight of the first representatives who responded this way. The difference is that all the more active original representatives had joined new groups, but only three of the more active new representatives had. The other two who were more active had not become members of new groups, but had merely gone to a great many more meetings of organizations than before.[25] Yet in spite of apparent differences in the magnitude of the change, the direction of the change is the same. Board membership activated the new community representatives even more than they had been activated by previous membership in poverty program organizations.

Before assessing the subjective and objective social mobility of the community representatives, we turn to consider the representatives' observations about board membership after six months of experience.

OBSERVATIONS OF THE NEW COMMUNITY
REPRESENTATIVES ON BOARD MEMBERSHIP

The comments of the new community representatives on board membership demonstrate the difficulty they had in working together and handling the pressures of their positions and also confirm that the representative's level of information, realism, and sophistication does increase. The representatives were no longer as frightened or as optimistic as they were in the original interview.

In the second interview the new community representatives were asked how much influence they felt the community representatives had had on the board. Their responses indicating that they had some influence were similar to those of the original representatives, as shown in table 25. One of the respondents who felt the community

TABLE 25

Community Representatives' Opinions of
Their Own Influence on the Board

Representatives	Influence	Some influence	Not much influence
Original	2	3	3
New	2	2	3

representatives had little influence cited an occasion when he made a suggestion, and said, "they say no like I'm stupid, I don't know what I'm talking about, but when an agency representative said the same thing there was a complete change, you know? Everybody is out to do what the agency man says because of where he works." The feeling among the three community representatives who responded negatively was that "we actually don't have as much power as we were set out to think we had . . . they are letting us have our say because it keeps the community quiet."

In the first interview all the representatives adamantly stated their desires to work closely together. And in early meetings, they repeatedly expressed the belief that unlike the original community representatives they would stick together. In their euphoria, many of them missed signs of internal tension which were easily apparent to observers. But in the second interview all acknowledged that definite splits had developed within the group, and they did not vote together as a bloc. A group of three feels close, several other community representatives are marginal members of this group, and the others are isolates.

The splits arose because of distrust among the representatives. There was mutual suspicion that community representatives were competing for leadership in order to use the board as a stepping-stone to advance themselves. They also commented that various representatives had become completely aligned with the establishment or really represented specific interests in the community.

The subgroupings and lack of trust among the new representatives are quite similar to the patterns found in the original community group. One difference is worth noting. The second group had more doubts about the competence of the other community representatives; they said certain representatives were ill-informed and plagued by personal problems which hindered their activities on the board.

In spite of the divisions among the community representatives, they like the original representatives got together before meetings and attempted to get support for issues. But the preplanning that did go on was not very effective. For example, shared anger about committee assignments was not translated into a strategy for changing the committees and a plan to present an alternative nomination for a board officer was not pursued.

The community representatives' responses to questions of influence and how the representatives worked together suggest an increase in information and realism. But this growth in sophistication is not as apparent when the representatives talk of keeping in touch with their constituents. There was, however, an increase in their awareness of community pressures. Three talked about attempts by community organizations to use the community representatives, to take advantage of them to promote the interests of the organizations. They cited instances of being told, if you do such and such "I will make it worth your while." Referring to pressures from the community organizations as well as from the agencies, one representative explained he had

gotten harder and colder: "You don't expect everybody is so innocent, nice, and sweet, don't trust everybody."

Like the original community representatives, these representatives indicated that the communications from the community are from
people related to the poverty programs, staff members or clients. The
new representatives did not talk as if they were getting as much communication as the old representatives did, and they did not seem to
be as bothered by what they got as the original representatives were.[26]
There were no changes in the community representatives' images of
what kind of board members they were.

Having considered the community representatives' descriptions
of board membership and their attitudes toward EYOA, it is possible
to formulate an answer to the question "Who did the community
representatives listen to?" All kinds of groups tried to get the community representatives on their side: these included the EYOA staff,
the agency representatives, staff members of delegate agencies, and
clients of poverty programs; and the representatives were used by different groups at different times. The original impression of their vul-
nerability was heightened after six months of observing them on the
board. In spite of personal increases in information and confidence,
the representatives lack unity, strategy, and a direction of their own.
They were not used by any one group but by a variety of groups.

The six training sessions they participated in did very little to
overcome these deficiencies, and in fact they illustrate the problem
well. The training sessions were designed and carried out by the staff.
They served to give the representatives information on how EYOA
functioned. But the sessions were aimed at transforming the community representatives into the staff's image of good board members,
namely, members who support the staff. No attempt was made to let
the old community representatives orient the new ones. No attention
was given to questions of strategies for gaining influence on the board.
In fact, any reference to issues of strategy and influence was met by
reprimands from the executive staff.

CHANGES IN CLASS: OBJECTIVE AND
SUBJECTIVE MOBILITY

Turning to a consideration of the mobility of the new community representatives, we find that the data provide interesting comparisons with the original community representatives and allow a fuller

understanding of what happens. Remember that the old community representatives experienced private upward social mobility but their orientations were still distinct from the downtown orientations of the agency representatives. The previous discussion of the changes in the attitudes of the new community representatives suggests that they too became less favorable to EYOA; they did not accept the agency representatives' positive evaluation of the organization. But we can now give a more thorough consideration to the question of social mobility, especially the issue of whether the new representatives exhibit the overconformity often linked with upward mobility.

In the first interview all the new representatives were asked whether they thought of themselves as middle class, working class, or lower class. Two stated unequivocally that they were part of the working class economically but that their value as people was "as high or higher than the city fathers." One of these explained: "Working class—that's all I've ever done, that's all I know how to do. Middle class people can play golf, canasta and bridge and stuff like that, you know. I don't have the time. I have to work." Two representatives identified themselves as lower class. One qualified his statement by saying that mentally he did not feel lower class: "I'm just not made that way. I say being poor doesn't mean being filthy." The three other representatives did not pick one of the choices offered. One explained: "To me there is no class at all. I can talk to a millionaire or a tramp. But I'm not upper class because I'm not a rich fellow. I'm a working man so I am middle class. Lower class are people on skid row, tramps." One said that he was not working class because he was not working right now, but he did not select the lower class label instead. He explained that he thought of himself as "above the average class of people" because he could speak with anyone and he likes it.

These responses suggest first that the representatives have a strong sense of personal worth apart from their economic position.[27] Second, the pattern suggests that even those who are publicly selected to be representatives of people in poverty do not on the whole identify themselves as lower class. They all distinguish themselves from people whom they see as lower than themselves in one sense or another. Bowen and Masotti also found that poverty candidates did not identify themselves with the poor and resisted discussing class differences.[28]

While six of the representatives did not identify themselves as lower class, the responses changed when the representatives were asked how similar they were to other poor people. Four indicated they thought of themselves as similar to other poor people. For example, one said he felt "we have this way of thinking because we live on the same level." But he distinguished between poor people and tramps. The three other community representatives indicated that they did not see themselves as similar to other poor people.[29]

Thus it is most interesting to find that when one analyzes responses about aspirations in the first interviews these same three community representatives are distinguished by ambitions to become upwardly mobile. It has already been stated (chapter 3) that most of the community representatives expressed a desire to improve themselves. But for four of the community representatives this self-improvement was not explicitly linked with a desire for improved status; they talked about getting into jobs which would provide support as they got older and working in their present community to improve it. But the three community representatives who characterized poor people as lazy talked in different terms. They talked of "going somewhere," of not just staying on the poverty board knocking themselves out, but going on to bigger things such as being a deputy for a politician or the politician himself. One explained: "I was the black sheep. . . . All my associates are something. I started thinking about it when my family was draggin' me down. I've got to start doing something or I'm going to go crazy. . . . If I could just get involved in things and let my friends see that I'm trying to do something, my friends up there in the hills." One described his desire for a house with a family room "where my kids can bring their friends home," a pool, basketball hoop on the garage, and tether ball in the yard. Some might say these representatives aspire to become middle class, but a more accurate description would be that they want to become part of the stable working class, the stable blue-collar workers.[30]

In the second interviews none of the community representatives indicated a change in class identification but several did talk about changes in their financial position. The economic situation had improved for two and worsened for two. One representative's spouse had gotten a job which was not a result of board membership and the other representative took a job with a delegate agency. The representatives who said their finances had deteriorated cited the same reasons as the original representatives did; the $25 a day of board business was inadequate and they could not find jobs that would permit them to continue fulfilling their board responsibilities.

There were no changes in the community representatives' identification with poor people. One explained that he was not concerned about whether his friends thought he was going middle class because "anybody who thinks that because a person tries to better himself and better others . . . he's middle class . . . it isn't true. Because I'm still living in the same community, same house, still no car." Later he added that he did not feel any different, it was just that opportunities for him were broader now.

But in spite of the lack of clear evidence of subjective or objective social mobility using the standard indications, the issue merits closer examination, as suggested in the representative's remarks about broader opportunities. The need for concentrating on the issue of class mobility is underlined by the expectations of the people who come into contact with the representatives. Community people, staff, and agency representatives often charge that community representatives quickly switch from a community to an establishment point of view. Many jokes are made about how rapidly community representatives learn to "play the game." Laughing references are made to their concern for obtaining calling cards, name markers, offices, phones, and as many per diem payments as possible.[31] The community representatives' defense is that they have to look out for their own survival. They point to the economic decline of some of the original community representatives. One explained: "You fight everybody else's troubles but there is nobody to fight your own troubles. Nobody can serve well when they have problems at home—how can you think straight when your gas is going to be cut off, and your child is hungry." They do not feel that concern with salaries or amenities makes them any less community people; they feel that such things are essential if they are going to effectively represent the community.

The interviews with the new community representatives did provide some evidence on the type of mobility which was taking place. The two major changes concerned self-esteem and aspirations. Every representative implied that board membership had increased his self-esteem. The representatives who said in the first interview that being on the board would test what kinds of people they were all indicated that they felt better about themselves. They said they had not been beaten down by the board and had proved to themselves that they would stick by their beliefs. One explained: "In spite of the headaches and stomach aches I get out of that board I think it is beautiful. I think I've never had a job that I could do better than this one. Where else could I really have fun and do my work at the same time?" Another explained that board membership made him feel better and kept him going and busy; he said, "I feel worthwhile, feel like a worthwhile person, you know, doing something," These signs of increase in positive self-image are very similar to the responses of the original community representatives.

Five out of the seven community representatives showed changes in their aspirations. The change was subtle but perhaps very significant and not primarily connected with improved social status. The most consistent change in aspiration was a new desire to become leaders in their communities. For example one individual who said in the first interview that he wanted to get into community work said in the second interview that he wanted to "have the power of connections to change things to make them better for other people." They talked about being spokesmen for their people, like Martin Luther King. For example, one representative who originally felt very afraid of not having enough to contribute to EYOA said: "I think there is more I can do than EYOA, just saying yes and no on something . . . like I'm a puppet and I don't like being a puppet . . . I want to change things. I want to work for the poor. . . . I even thought of starting my own organization of poor people." The changes in aspiration were paralleled by the representatives' increased sense of political efficacy, which has already been discussed.

Three of the five community representatives who aspired to become leaders described specific steps they were going to follow to fulfill their goals. Two clearly saw themselves as eventually becoming professionals in community work. They said they were becoming more professional and referred to academic work they would pursue. The third felt he could not fit in established social agencies and would be fired for criticizing them. Instead he wanted to get into an organization that "really moves," that really changes things for the poor, such as the Welfare Rights Organization. One of the other representatives who saw himself as a leader had no specific plans for himself, but one of his children had been influenced by his parent's aspirations, becoming very active in protest activities and deciding to go to college and prepare for community organization work so that he could be even more of a leader than his parent.

In several of the cases one wonders, however, if the new aspirations are realistic. During the first six months on the board these representatives had family and health problems related to the unfamiliar stresses of board membership. They also seemed to have the least self-awareness and personal security. In the interviews they tended to say the "right" thing and to suppress other feelings that were shown nevertheless in contradictory statements. For example, one said he respected politicians because "they are servants of the people" but later said they were a "bunch of skunks" because they "don't listen to our wants and needs."

In general, however, the changes in self-image as shown by changes in self-esteem and aspirations suggest that the experience of the new representatives will parallel that of the original representatives. Chapter 5 argued that board membership influenced the original representatives to become more active in the community. Closer analysis of the new representatives indicates that underlying this change there is an important change in self-image. Individuals are not only activated but see themselves as potential leaders in their communities.[32]

Furthermore, the data on the new representatives support the argument that the changes in the community representatives do not result in their becoming so similar to the agency representatives that they lose their community orientation. Board membership for the new representatives, as for the old representatives, seems to be a transitional step in private upward social mobility, but the mobility involves a change from unstable lower class to stable lower or stable working class, from insecurity and self-doubts to feelings of security and personal worth. But the most important change is from inactive followers to more active leaders within the poverty community.

Little evidence exists that the type of upward mobility these representatives were experiencing involved overconformity.[33] They did not identify with the values of the agency people before being on the board or after.[34] They were not militantly alienated poor before they got on the board but neither were they moderate allegiants. They were similar to the agency representatives in some ways, as in accepting their view of the role of community representatives, but they were distinguished in many ways, as in their views on the agencies and militant protest. Some of their changes after being on the board made them more similar to agency representatives—they gained more information, more understanding of agency members, and more confidence; but some of their changes made them more distinct, namely their increased hostility toward EYOA and their desire to bring about change in their own communities. So after they had been on the board they were still neither militantly alienated nor moderately allegiant. Insofar as there is similarity to the agency people prior to being on the board, the mechanism at work seems to be self-selection and early political socialization.[35] The similarities after being on the board are the result of socialization but the socialization is selective. The community representatives did not attempt to become identical with the agency representatives. They tried to become more equal in power but separate. Their experience emphasizes the emergence of the new role which has been called here the professional poor person. This role may be ridiculed by both poor people and established professionals as simply a middle-class phenomenon, but it is actually something different.

OVERVIEW OF CHANGES IN COMMUNITY REPRESENTATIVES

The data on the changes in the new community representatives make possible some generalizations about the effect of board membership on both sets of community representatives, and speculation on the reasons why different representatives changed in the directions they did, and on the relative effectiveness of different types of members and the two groups of representatives.

Study of the two different groups of community representatives suggests that in general the socialization in both groups was quite similar. The most frequently mentioned change in each was an increase in information and understanding about how EYOA operates. And in both there was an increase in personal confidence and in positive feelings about the agency representatives on the board. But these attitudes do not carry over into more positive attitudes toward EYOA or the agencies involved. Both sets of representatives became more disillusioned with EYOA, and their preexisting attitudes toward the agencies did not become more positive except toward the schools. Both groups had become more active in the community and interested in careers in community work. The new representatives showed clear increases in political efficacy, positive feelings toward the federal government, and self-esteem and leadership aspirations. These were not as clear among the original representatives, probably because of differences in method. Neither group showed much change in attitudes toward militancy or the political parties.

The increases in confidence, efficacy, participation, interest in community work, self-esteem and leadership aspirations mark a major change in the community representatives' political socialization and may have a significant impact on the people and organizations with whom they come into contact.

Observation of the new representatives over six months serves to underscore the difficulty of explaining why the individuals changed in the ways they did. The impression of the representatives at the time of the first interviews was that they were very vulnerable and could go in many different directions. In retrospect, one continues to feel that they could have gone in different directions. Ambition for upward mobility did not prove to be a reliable indicator of behavior. The three individuals with the clearest desires for improved status did not become more favorable to EYOA or less abrasive. Similarly the career plans of the representatives did not prove to be a useful way of explaining the changes on the board.[36] The individuals who appeared most insecure personally did prove to be the most erratic, easily swayed by others, and adamant about one position then equally adamant about a contradictory position with apparent unawareness of what they were doing. But the key factor in how these individuals changed was apparently the internal dynamics by which the individuals established their relative power within the group. Individuals who felt rebuffed by or insecure in the group became bitter toward EYOA and suspicious of the other representatives. They saw themselves as loners.[37] The most important differentiator among the representatives was their ability to work with the other community representatives. While this ability was not apparent in the interviews, it became apparent in the first months of their interaction. The leaders and the followers became distinguished as well as those who were set apart from the group. The leaders were those who combined competence in EYOA procedures with more ability to get along with community people and the agency representatives.[38]

The pattern of leadership also suggests an answer to the question of what types of representatives are most effective on the EYOA board. In both groups the community representatives rated by other board members as most influential also appeared most effective. The style of operation was different in each case, one more aggressive, one more conciliatory, but in each case they were recognized by other representatives as sharp, competent, informed, and as having powerful links in the community. One was suspected by some as being pro establishment, the other never was, and some community representatives questioned their motives but no one questioned their determination to win and their relative competence at using strategy to get close to their goals.

What can be said about the relative influence of the two groups of community representatives on the functioning of the board? A major thesis of this research is that both groups have had a similarly low level of influence (see chapter 4). Some people feel the new group has had more influence, others feel that the original group did. The conclusion of this observer is that whatever differences in influence there are do not relate to differences in the types of representatives recruited. The fact that the new representatives had had more experience in poverty organizations than the original ones did not significantly increase their effectiveness on the board. But neither did this previous involvement make them more positive to EYOA or more oriented toward the establishment and thus less likely to present a view from the community. The new group, like the old group, saw their job as speaking for the little man. Any differences in influence seem more related to other changes occurring at EYOA, namely in the executive director and his staff, in the concerns of the public agencies which resulted in their appointing lower level men to sit on the EYOA board, and in the decline of community action projects. These changes together help explain the agency's loss of vitality as the focus of attention moved away from community action programs. The major battles among the interests in Los Angeles no longer swirl around EYOA; the pattern has been set and the hopes for major changes have faded. Within this context any gain in influence by community representatives, such as their success in originating hearings into irregularities in delegate agencies, must be seen as more apparent than real. The gain is merely an indicator of the willingness of the public agencies to go along. Future influence of community representatives on the operation of the board will depend largely on a revitalization of the agency and a redefinition of its goals and purposes. Much of this will depend on forces external to EYOA.

III: CONCLUSION
★ ★ ★ ★ ★ ★ ★

7. Implications for Theory and Policy

This study of the board members of the Economic and Youth Opportunities Agency of Greater Los Angeles started with the question of what happens when poor people become members of the board. In closing, the main outlines of the answer to that question are reviewed. Then attention is given to the implications of the findings for theory and public policy.

The results of the present study indicate that community representatives on the EYOA were co-opted. They did not gain power over the decisions made by the board, or diminish the public agencies' predominant influence on the board. But when one turns from an organizational to an individual level of analysis, the results are somewhat different. That is, one must distinguish between the effect of the participation of the poor on the board and its effect on the socialization of the individual board members. The community representatives were activated by their experiences on the board so that their level of participation in the political system was raised. This change is indicated by the increases in personal and political efficacy, understanding of how the board operates, organizational participation, aspirations to do community work, and images of themselves as leaders. The fact that these changes are not accompanied by an increase in positive feelings toward EYOA and other local public agencies suggests that the activated community representatives have not become merely defenders of the status quo. The community representatives continue to be distinguished from the other board members by their greater dissatisfaction with established patterns of dealing with poverty and their interest in faster change. Leaders for social change are not being siphoned off by the poverty program; they are being created where they did not exist before. The agency representatives were also changed by the participation of community representatives on the board. They became somewhat more aware and tolerant of the community point of view, but they did not change as much as the poverty members.

The positive aspects of participation of the poor on the Los Angeles board are not an argument for retaining the current system. The changes in socialization do not compensate for the powerlessness of the representatives or for their being used to quiet the community. But the positive aspects are an argument for weighing any alternative to ascertain its effects on socialization. Those who want rapid power for the poor may give unintended support to opponents of this power by suggesting it would be better to eliminate community participation rather than have powerless participation. The argument here is that some participation is better than no participation. Access to the decision-making process without power to determine the outcome is better than no access.[1] Experience on the board gives the community representatives more skill, confidence, and involvement without eliminating their poverty perspective. So their ability to serve as sources of change is enhanced even though they do not succeed in immediately changing the direction of EYOA and the public agencies. Furthermore, the community representatives do have an effect on some board decisions when the agency representatives are willing; they speak for interests that might otherwise not be heard. And their presence somewhat changes the attitudes of the agency representatives.

IMPLICATIONS FOR THEORY

Throughout this study an attempt has been made to relate the findings to social science literature, but it is useful to summarize the main theoretical implications. The study has implications for several aspects of social science, notably participation, socialization, urban politics, and federalism. Since all cannot be discussed here, emphasis is placed on the two aspects that seem most significant, participation and socialization. Obviously the generalizations from any case study must be viewed with caution; they are only suggestive and should serve as stimuli for further testing.

Implications for the Study of Participation

The characteristics of the agency representatives and community representatives reflect the differences in their recruitment. The community representatives are differentiated from the agency representatives by socioeconomic and attitudinal characteristics associated with lower or working classes. The EYOA election system recruits individuals with limited participation in community organizations. They belong to more organizations than would be expected of low income people, but they have not been leaders in community organizations and have no prior experience with organizations operating at the policy level of EYOA, so participation on the board does mark a change in their participation patterns.

The recruitment of community representatives indicates that Almond and Verba's formulation of the causes of participation[2] is not adequate for explaining why the community representatives changed their participation patterns to get involved in poverty programs and the board. Furthermore, the switch from withdrawal to participation was not related to either satisfaction or dissatisfaction with the political system. Instead it involved the convergence of personal needs and ego strength with easy availability, especially when these were accompanied by personal invitations to participate.

Present social theory is not very helpful in explaining many aspects of the community representatives. It does not begin to describe the variety of life styles among the poor or measure the prevalence of the different styles. Thus one finds it difficult to know where the community representatives fit. They can be placed in existing typologies such as allegiant-alienated or stable-unstable but mere classification is not very useful. One wants to know, for example, what poor people in the real world would also be found in the same position, are there many such people, and how does ethnicity relate to that position? Data on the community representatives suggest that the majority of them suffer economic instability and that half of these have family instability as well. Thus they can be categorized as unstable poor or copers. They are neither extremely alienated militants nor allegiant moderates. Like *Tally's Corner* people, they exhibit erratic employment patterns and are in the limbo between the stable lower middle working class and the derelicts.[3] But none of the representatives in this category is a Negro male and other details of their lives also vary markedly from the *Tally's Corner* men. There is a lack of studies of the life styles of poor Negro women and Mexican-American men and women in urban America which might provide useful standards against which to compare community representatives.

Study of the functioning of the board supports the findings of Marris and Rein, Greenstone and Peterson, and Selznick on the powerlessness of the poor when added to governing boards.[4] While the community representatives are formally equal participants and in fact do participate actively in the discussions and work of this policy-making board, they have not gained power on it. They have been co-opted. Change in participation patterns is not necessarily linked with a change in the power of participants. In Los Angeles the addition of community representatives did not change the preexisting positions of the groups in the policy arena. It was an innovation in the form of policy-making but not a change in the balance of power, and it did not have a major impact on the content of policy. The addition of new participants to the decision-making body, however, had some marginal effects on policy when the agency representatives were in agreement, and it brought a new viewpoint to the board.[5]

The difficulty in determining the power balance at EYOA using either the reputational or the decisional approaches emphasizes the need for social scientists to consider how to measure the "other face of power"[6] where implicit influence limits controversy. This type of influence makes it difficult to evaluate the effectiveness of community participation on the board. The community representatives appear to effect certain decisions but only when the public agencies are willing.

Implications for the Study of Socialization

The crucial issue in the present study is the relationship between participation and socialization, particularly increases in efficacy and affect. Participation on a poverty board which marked an increase in participation for the community representatives is linked with an increase in efficacy. But increases in participation and efficacy are not connected with increases in affect toward EYOA. The experience on the board did not make the community representatives more allegiant or moderate but actually made them more negative toward the agency. This finding challenges the expectation that participation and efficacy are linked with positive affect. Existing social theory has not yet shown how this disparity can be explained. More attention must clearly be given to specifying the conditions under which participation and efficacy are linked with positive evaluations and with negative ones. Two of the key variables appear to be the subjective interests of the individuals and the nature of the organization that they are evaluating. The increased information and confidence that can come from participation may lead to a more realistic awareness of the inability of the environment to meet one's own needs and thus to a more negative opinion of that environment.

A major theme implicit in this whole analysis of participation is that the socialization of the poverty representatives makes them more aware of their latent interests and thus increases their conflict with the boards. Such conflict, rather than being disruptive of a stable integrated social system, is seen as a potentially important component of social change.[7] The changes in the agency representatives support the idea that the attitudes of those "on top" help account for the attitudes of those below them.[8] A noticeable perception gap exists between the agency and community representatives. While the agency representatives closed the gap somewhat by becoming more understanding of the community representatives, the depth of these changes is not clear. Their roles in their own agencies were not modified. None acknowledged that attacks on poverty might necessitate changes in the power balance and few became more sympathetic to conflict as an essential part of change.

The changes in attitudes that took place among board members suggest that more systematic attention should be given to the impact of organizational membership on adult socialization. The agency representatives did not undergo basic changes in political orientation; they had more experience in organizations and their roles on the board were structured by the agencies they represented. But for the poverty representatives the experience marks a significant change in political behavior, a turning point in their lives.[9] Poverty organizations ought not to be looked at solely as mechanisms for efficient job performance, but also as mechanisms for socialization. They are arenas in which political attitudes are being shaped, loyalties and self-images are being influenced. There is as yet markedly little attention being given to this aspect of the organizations by scholars or by participants. As a result, many of those involved are insensitive to the impact the experience is having on the participants.

An important question about the participation and socialization patterns summarized here is the extent to which they are a function of the war on poverty and Los Angeles politics. Even though the data are not adequate, speculation is possible. Los Angeles politics certainly is a prime influence on the power relationships found in EYOA.

The relative importance of the public agencies in Los Angeles' decentralized, fragmented political system helped them shape EYOA to protect their interests and to ensure that the community representatives on the board would be inexperienced individuals without a power base. Thus very little dispersion of power to the poor took place in the reform city of Los Angeles.[10] But power dispersion also was absent in cities with different political systems, such as Chicago and Boston.[11] So while Los Angeles' political system was a primary variable, other political systems could experience the same result, and it is important to specify and compare the mechanisms operating in these diverse settings.[12]

While the power balance in EYOA reflects the Los Angeles political system, indications are that at least some aspects of the socialization taking place on EYOA are duplicated on CAA boards throughout the country.[13] No matter what the structure of the boards it seems likely that community representatives will show increased feelings of efficacy. On the other hand, hostility to CAA does not always increase; this change seems to be related to the amount of power the community representatives feel they have on the board and their level of expectation.

The evidence that does exist suggests that the power balance and the socialization patterns at EYOA are not primarily a function of the war on poverty. Similar patterns emerge in a wide variety of social programs.[14] Intervention by the national government in such programs as health, housing, and education typically reinforces the existing local political patterns.[15] In all these programs some attention is given to community participation and whenever a power differential exists between the people working together certain trends emerge: the persistence of the preexisting power balance, a gradual increase in the willingness of the powerful to be understanding of the intruders without transferring power, a change in the aspirations of the powerless owing to change in their associations. We need to look at the diverse programs more closely to discover under what conditions such trends emerge. For example, how does the situation of nonprofessional educational and medical aides differ from that of poor people on school and medical advisory groups? Under what circumstances are changes in the power balance maximized and professionals made more receptive to nonprofessionals? Does conflict help or hinder the changes?

Comparison of the conditions found at EYOA with the growing evidence from other programs adds to the belief that the situation described in this case study may be indicative of trends in cities throughout the United States and in a wide variety of federally funded programs. The boundary conditions producing the patterns described here are not unique to Los Angeles or the war on poverty. Systematic comparative studies and syntheses of existing data on individual cities and programs are sorely needed.

POLICY IMPLICATIONS

The foregoing summary of this study's theoretical implications can serve as a basis for many different types of policy recommendations depending on one's assumptions and values. The assumption here is that owing to the rising discontent with the existing power balance in the United States, the danger of making it possible for the poor to gain more power is not as great as the danger of not making it possible. (The danger is not that they cannot be put down but that the repression will destroy the democratic system.)

The addition of poor people to decision-making boards has not proved to be an effective way for the poor to gain more power in the short run. The tone of this study, as of the studies cited in chapter 1, has been pessimistic. Contrary to the fears of local officials, the presence of poverty representatives on community action agencies has not meant that they have taken over city halls. The poor have not destroyed the system, they have simply been "spuriously involved." This token involvement has meant that local agencies have missed a chance to increase their sensitivity to local needs.[16] And the national trend clearly continues away from the idea of community action by involving the poor.

But what does the accumulated evidence from the war on poverty suggest about ways the poor could gain power? First it suggests that attempts to use public funds to organize the poor can only be marginally successful in the short run, and cannot be relied upon to do the major part of the work. As elected officials became aware that community action might involve organizing sources of possible opposition, community action was emasculated. Even the addition of poverty representatives to city-wide boards can be seen as a substitute for radical forms of community participation which would have meant that local communities within cities would have been involved in the actual determination of what they wanted.[17] Second, it suggests that the plan to funnel all funds to only one umbrella agency in a locality makes it even more unlikely that organization of the poor will occur. The concept of having one coordinating board appeals to rational administrative principles but the result of this plan is that all the existing power groups focus their attention on this one entity and succeed in making it reflect the existing power balance.

Marris and Rein, in *Dilemmas of Social Reform,* argue that the goals of coordination and community organization are in conflict. The conclusion is that the federal government "should be prepared to support, in the same community, both official and countervailing conceptions of a viable programme."[18] And in addition philanthropic groups should support unofficial poverty programs which could develop alternative approaches not limited by political considerations and which would serve as standards of comparison for the public efforts. This approach may be thought of as "competition in the public interest."[19]

Yet while this major change in direction offers some interesting possibilities for more effective organization of the poor, there are some piecemeal changes in the existing community action agencies which offer stopgap ways of strengthening participation. In Los Angeles the most important immediate changes would be the organization of local area councils in poverty pockets and the revision of the election system so that the representatives are elected by area councils and have an organized constituency.[20] The fact that there are difficulties connected with the various plans for implementing these changes should no longer be used as an excuse for avoiding any change at all.[21] The existing system is entirely inadequate for genuine community action so any change in the direction of linking the EYOA board and the community representatives with neighborhood organizations will be an improvement. If this linkage is made area councils should be able to elect any person they wish as their representative to the EYOA board and the $4,000 criteria for community representatives should be removed.

There are ways to strengthen community representatives, however, no matter how they are elected. One way involves making genuine training available to them.[22] It is true that the EYOA staff provided seven extended training sessions for the new representatives and made some minor efforts to orient the original representatives. But the content of the training, while useful to the representatives in giving them information on how things are done at EYOA, was geared toward "fitting them into the board." The stress was on making them good team members, teaching them that a good board works through the executive director and does not interfere with the staff. Bloc voting was specifically discouraged. The assumption behind the training was that the board should function like the board of directors of a private corporation rather than as a representative body; public spirited individuals were to reason together in a spirit of consensus and come up with decisions in the public interest. As a result no explicit consideration was given to the strategies of being influential with the board and staff, of lobbying, of mobilizing support for an issue. There was no discussion of the advantages and disadvantages of working as a group, of when it is possible and when it is not, of the possibilities of logrolling. No attempt was made to analyze the conflicting viewpoint and interests of the staff and other board members. No group dynamics or sensitivity training was given.

It seems unrealistic to expect these aspects to be dealt with by the staff. Many of them are necessarily interested in having a board that interferes as little as possible with their activities. Other staff members would like to use the community representatives as weapons in their fight against the public agencies. In any case when the staff runs sessions they have a point of view to sell. Thus it seems imperative that training of the community representatives be done by some other group than the EYOA staff, preferably an independent training group. A variety of such groups exist, although all of them would also have points of view. But since they would not be formally linked to EYOA, they might raise more of the questions that need to be raised.[23]

The community representatives should select the training group themselves and change contractors if they are not satisfied with the services they get.[24] The training should include an on-going consulting service with experienced individuals including former community representatives to whom the representatives could turn for advice as issues arise on the board. This kind of support would seem to be valuable even if the community representatives were linked with neighborhood councils who were giving them support. The training group could provide an alternative view.

The suggestion of training for community representatives might imply that the agency representatives do not need such training. This is not the case. The board and the agency are in great need of redefinition of goals, roles, and priorities. Several days of concentrated informal discussions might give the board and the agency a new sense of direction. The difficulty is that some of the people involved do not feel such sessions would be productive enough to merit giving up the time it would require away from their other responsibilities.[25] Yet if the community representatives are receiving training, the others may insist that the training not be separate, because that might set the community representatives against the rest of the board. Such insistence could lead to joint sessions at which the dialogue could be very interesting.

Even if training is not provided and the election system is not revised, there are ways the community representatives could be strengthened. The role of community representatives must be clarified. Are they ombudsmen for the poverty program or representatives of the poverty community? In either case they must be given more support in carrying out their role. Support might include offices, more staff assistance, and salaries rather than per diem payments.[26]

And without any increase in expenses the community representatives could strengthen their own position on the board. They could have regular caucuses to decide what they are for and to plan strategies for furthering their goals. Finding areas of agreement will not be easy but it will give them a stronger voice on the board. It will enable them to resist the manipulation of their votes which makes them appear to have been won over by the agency representatives. Agreement on specific issues and strategies should also make them feel freer to resist the internal culture of the board and bring up more issues of controversy. Two ways to indicate a determination to work together when possible would be to elect a chairman and vice chairman of their caucus and to call press conferences to clarify their positions on issues.[27]

In spite of the difficulties in all suggestions for increasing the power of the poor, and in spite of the national trend away from organizing the poor, conversation with the community representatives confirms that the idea will not die out. The changes may come more or less rapidly, more or less violently, but changes in attitude and behavior are occurring which suggest that changes in the power balance are possible.

CONCLUDING REFLECTIONS

This exploratory study of a CAA board suggests many directions for further work. A follow-up study is needed of the depth and persistence of the changes in the board members. Do the community representatives stay activated? Do they serve as leaders for social change in their communities? One wonders, too, how the staff members of delegate agencies who urged the representatives to run for election and the people in the communities see the representatives and their changes. Comparative studies are also needed to determine the extent to which the members of other poverty boards and the participants in other federally funded social programs exhibit similar patterns of change.

A case study of thirty-two people can be enlightening in an era when the social sciences are fraught with methodological discussions of theoretical frameworks, sample surveys focused on large cross sections of the population, multiple regression and systems analysis. Consideration of the broad system can be useful and so can a closer look at a small arena. The latter shows how misleading social science generalizations can be when applied to certain cases and provides the chance to revise these concepts so they will more adequately reflect reality. Case studies also suggest some of the dynamics that may be operating behind the static correlations.

It has been enjoyable, too, to find that CAA board members bear only a dim resemblance to the depressing picture of alienated minorities and organization men in social science literature. The community representatives are neither innocent creatures cruelly exploited nor sullen beasts intent upon destroying the American way. The agency representatives are neither evil manipulators nor all wise leaders. The board members are acted upon by forces they cannot control and are also able to act in ways that do change the forces. They are experiencing in individual terms some of the forces characteristic of our era—the discontent of blacks, browns, and the poor; the schemes of social reformers; the growth of governmental intervention and new approaches to policy-making. All these forces swirl around the issue of the participation of the poor. The individuals caught in this political maelstrom manifesting itself on CAA boards may not be doing well at handling it, but at least they are making a start. And starting is important.

Furthermore, there are steps that both the agency and community representatives can take to make the participation of the poor more important. The agency representatives can bring questions into the open about the goals of CAAs and the roles of board members. They can face the question of whether their new understanding of community representatives is superficial and transitory. The answer to this will depend upon their willingness to allow the poor to obtain the minimal tools they need to become more equal on boards. The community representatives can formulate their own goals and roles and work toward them with more confidence. Certainly they will be criticized by the poor and the professionals; board membership makes them distinct from both groups. But if their activation as leaders in their communities continues, they can serve as sources of change.

The poverty representatives described in the opening paragraphs of this study have changed. The twice-divorced woman with six children is no longer on welfare. She is a vocal staff member of a war on poverty program and active on a model cities citizen's advisory board. The woman who had never registered to vote until she joined the board is now a leader in an organization urging people to organize to gain political influence and she has been appointed to a task force to study Head Start.

Such activation appears to be the only alternative to the present co-optation. In the short run, community representatives are co-opted, but in the long run, if they resist being won over and maintain their identity with the poor community, they can work for the day when co-optation of the poor will no longer be so easy because the poor will have equal access to political power and to the resulting benefits of meaningful participation in the changing political system.

APPENDIXES

★ ★ ★ ★ ★ ★

I. Interview Checklists and Background Questionnaire

Note: The interviews will be nonstructured but the following list of topics and questions indicate the focus of the interviews and serves as a checklist to ensure that the topics are covered.

I. Recruitment
  A. How they got on the board.
       How did they hear of the war on poverty and EYOA?
       How did they happen to run?
       How did they campaign? What people and groups helped them? Who voted for them?
  B. Why they think other members got on the board.
       Why do they think other community representatives got involved?
       Why do they think other board members got involved?

II. Behavior prior to participation on the board.
  A. Attitudes toward EYOA prior to their involvement.
       What did they think EYOA ought to do? What did they see as the job of the board? What did they think about the inclusion of community representatives?
       What were their expectations about whom they would represent and what their constituents expected?
       What were their expectations about how they would relate to the Board and what contacts they would have with other members, especially the community representatives?
  B. Other relevant attitudes
       How good a job did they think the following were doing to help the poor: school system, county (for example, welfare and

probation), city, and voluntary agencies such as churches and settlements.

How interested were they in local affairs? State? National? (For example, did they follow the elections and vote?)

How much influence did they think an individual could have on local, state, and national affairs?

What did they feel about how much change is needed and how it could be brought about?

How militant were they personally?

C. Participation

How active were they in community affairs?

How did they get involved?

What past experiences were relevant to their involvement?

How similar did they used to be to other poor people?

III. Functioning of the board

A. Nature of participation on the board

What are their views of how they have participated on the board? How much influence have they had on board decisions? How important has membership been to them?

Are there individuals on the board that they tend to agree with or disagree with most of the time?

Are there individuals on the board who have particular influence over board decisions? Are there people or groups outside the board who have particular influence over decisions made by the board?

How much do they interact with board members outside of meetings? How much do they think others interact?

B. Key decisions of the board

What have the key decisions of the board consisted of?

How has the board been divided on these issues and why? Why did they themselves take the positions they did? What positions did other community representatives take?

C. Community representatives

What effect have the community representatives had on the board? Have they had any influence on the decisions of the board?

How do the community representatives vote?

What are their own reactions to the other community representatives? What do they think are the reactions of the other members to the community representatives?

Why wasn't there a fight when the number of community representatives was increased from seven to eight?

D. Relations between the representatives and their constituents

What did their constituents think about the positions they took on the board? How do they hear from and communicate with their constituents? Who are their supporters? Who are their critics?

IV. Behavior after participation on the EYOA board

A. Attitudes toward EYOA

What do they think of the way EYOA and the board have actually operated?

Are there people or groups not getting enough influence?
Are there people or groups getting too much influence?
Are there poverty programs they think are getting too much money? Too little money?
What are their impressions of the other board members and the staff?

What do they think are the attitudes of the other members toward EYOA and the board?

B. What do they see as the major changes in their attitudes as a result of being on the board?

What do they feel now about the job the following are doing to help the poor: school system, county, city, and voluntary agencies.

How interested are they now in local, state, and national affairs?
How much influence do they now think an individual can have on local, state, and national affairs?
What do they feel now about how much change is needed and how it can be brought about?
How militant are they now?
What has happened to their attitudes toward involving poor people in the war on poverty?
How active are they now in community affairs?
How similar are they now to other poor people?

C. What changes have they seen in the other board members?

D. What are their hopes for themselves two years from now? Type of job? Income? Education?

E. What effect did being on the board have on their community's opinion of them?

F. What help or training do they think would improve the functioning of the board?

G. Additional comments or suggestions for other questions to ask?

B. NEWLY ELECTED COMMUNITY REPRESENTATIVES
ON EYOA BOARD INTERVIEW CHECKLIST

I. Recruitment

How did they hear of the war on poverty and EYOA?
How have they been involved in it? How did they get involved?
How did they happen to run?

How did they campaign? What people and groups helped them? Who voted for them?

What do they know about their main competitors? Why did they run? Who supported them?

What do they know about the other newly elected community representatives?

II. Behavior prior to participation on the EYOA board

  A. Attitudes toward EYOA

What do they think EYOA ought to do? What should the board do? What part should poor people play in the war on poverty?

What do they think of the way EYOA and the board have actually operated?

    Are there people or groups that have particular influence with EYOA? Are there people or groups not getting enough influence?

    Are there poverty programs they think are getting too much money? Too little money?

    What are their impressions of the former community representatives? The other board members? And the staff?

Whom do they expect to represent on the board? How do they plan to relate to their constituents? What do they think their constituents expect of them?

How do they expect to operate on the board? What contact with the other community representatives?

  B. Other relevant attitudes

How good a job do they think the following are doing to help the poor: School system, county (for example, welfare and probation), city, voluntary agencies such as churches and settlements.

How interested have they been in local affairs? State? National? For example, did they follow the elections and vote?

How much influence do they think an individual can have on local, state, and national affairs? (Do public officials listen? Can ordinary people understand and have any say? For example, if a local ruling was being made that you considered unjust, what do you think you could do? How likely is it that you would succeed? How likely that you would try? Have you tried?)

What do they feel about how much change is needed? How should it be brought about? (Source of change—local, state, national, or private effort. Method of change—how much conflict and fighting, lawbreaking? For example, do they feel the following are ever justified: picketing, school boycotts, sit-ins?)

How militant are they personally? For example, do they identify with Malcolm X or Martin Luther King? Chavez or
Tijerina?

C. Participation

How active are they in community affairs?

How did they get involved?

What past experiences were relevant to their involvement?

III. Expectations

How similar do they think they are to other poor people?

What are their hopes for themselves two years from now? Type of
job? Income? Education?

What effect do they think being on the board will have on their
opinions?

What effect do they think being on the board will have on their
community's opinion of them?

Additional comments on their views or suggestions for other questions
which should be asked?

C. OTHER MEMBERS OF THE EYOA BOARD
INTERVIEW CHECKLIST

I. Recruitment

A. How they got on the board. Why were they chosen by their organization? How did they get into the position that made them
eligible?

B. Why they think other members got on the board. Why do they
think others from their own agency and from other agencies
got involved? Why do they think the community representatives
got involved?

II. Behavior prior to participation on the board

A. Attitudes toward EYOA prior to their involvement.

What did they think EYOA ought to do? What did they see
as the job of the board? What did they think about the inclusion of community representatives?

What were their expectations about whom they would represent, and what their organizations would require?

What were their expectations about how they would relate to
the board and what contacts they would have with other
members?

III. Functioning of the board

A. Nature of participation on the board

What are their views of how they have participated on the
board? How much influence have they had on board
decisions? How important has membership been to them?

Are there individuals on the board that they tend to agree with or disagree with most of the time?

Are there individuals who have particular influence over the decisions made by the board? Are there people or groups outside the board who have particular influence over decisions made by the board?

How much do they interact with board members outside of meetings? How much do they think others interact?

B. Key decisions of the board

What have the key decisions of the board consisted of?

How has the board been divided on these issues and why? Why did they themselves take the positions they did? What positions did others from the same organization take?

C. Community representatives

What effect have the community representatives had on the board? Have they had any influence on the decisions of the board? Examples? What problems have they created (for example, undue deference, increased debating time with little change in results)?

How do the community representatives vote?

What are their own reactions to the community representatives? What do they think are the reactions of the other members to the community representatives?

Why wasn't there a fight when the number of community representatives was increased from seven to eight?

D. Relations between the members and their organizations

On what issues do they get instructions and reactions from their agencies?

What effect has participation on the EYOA board had on their agencies? Changes in procedures, staff, objectives, and relations with other agencies?

IV. Behavior after participation on the EYOA board

A. Attitudes toward EYOA

What do they think of the way EYOA and the board have actually operated?

Are there people or groups not getting enough influence?

Are there people or groups getting too much influence?

Are there poverty programs they think are getting too much money? Too little money?

What are their impressions of the other board members and the staff?

What do they think are the attitudes of the other board members toward EYOA and the board?

B. What do they see as the major changes in their attitudes as a result of being on the board?

What has happened to their attitudes toward social change?
How much is needed and what kind?
Where is the needed change most likely to come from?
Local, state, national, or private effort?
What methods of bringing about change are acceptable?
How much conflict, fighting, lawbreaking? For example, do they feel the following are ever justified—picketing, school boycotts, sit-ins?
How militant are they personally?
Do they think of themselves as liberals or conservatives?
What has happened to their attitudes toward involving poor people in the war on poverty?
What has happened to their picture of their own agency (and its relations with other agencies and the community) and their own relation to their agency?

C. What changes have they seen in the other board members including the community representatives?
D. What kind of job would they like to have two years from now?
E. What help or training do they think would improve the functioning of the board?
F. Additional comments on the functioning of the board and suggestions for other questions that should be asked.

D. EYOA BOARD BACKGROUND QUESTIONNAIRE

Name _____ Home Address _____

1. What other areas of Los Angeles have you lived in besides your current area? (List in order from "most recent" to "least recent") _____

_____

2. (a) How many years have you lived in the Los Angeles area? _____
   (b) If not entire life, before coming to the Los Angeles area, where did you live? (List the main places, including name of town and state, in order from "most recent" to "least recent.")

_____

3. Did you grow up __ on a farm, __ in a small town, __ in a suburban area, or __ big city?

4. What were the political party preferences of your parents when you were growing up?
   Father: __ Democrat __ Republican __ Independent __ Other
   Mother: __ Democrat __ Republican __ Independent __ Other

5. How interested in politics were your parents when you were growing up?

Father: __ Very interested __ Somewhat interested
— Hardly at all
Mother: __ Very interested __ Somewhat interested
— Hardly at all

6. How active in community affairs were your parents when you were growing up?
Father: __ Very prominent __ Quite active __ Somewhat active
__ Hardly active
Mother: __ Very prominent __ Quite active __ Somewhat active
__ Hardly active

7. (a) At that time, what kind of work did your father do?

_____

(b) What kind of work did your mother do? _____

8. (a) What was the last grade your father completed in school? _____
(b) What was the last grade your mother completed in school? _____

9. In what year were you born? _____

10. How many brothers and sisters do you have? _____

11. (a) What is your religious background? __ Protestant __ Catholic
__ Jewish — Other
(b) How often do you attend services? __ Regularly __ Occasionally
__ Seldom __ Never

12. (a) Are you married or not? __ Married __ Widowed __ Divorced
__ Separated __ Single
(b) If you have children please list their ages _____

13. Do you own your home or rent it? __ own __ rent

14. Which of the following comes closest to describing the social class you would say you belong to? __ Upper class __ Upper middle class
__ Middle class __ Working class __ Lower class

15. About how much income did you and the members of your immediate family living in your house make last year before taxes?
__ Under $4,000   __ $ 4,000–$ 6,000 __ $ 7,000–$ 9,000
__ $10,000–$12,000   __ $13,000–$15,000 __ $16,000–$18,000
__ $19,000–$21,000   __ $22,000–$24,000 __ $25,000–$27,000
__ $28,000–$30,000   __ $31,000–$35,000 __ $36,000–$40,000
__ Above $40,000.

16. How likely is it that you will move away from the Los Angeles area in the next ten years? __ Quite likely __ Somewhat likely
__ Rather likely __ Rather unlikely.

17. (a) What was the highest grade of school you completed: _____
(b) If higher than 12th grade, please list the colleges you attended,

the dates of attendance, the degrees you received, and your major.
(List in order from "most recent" to "least recent.")
College   Dates   Degree   Major

_____

_____

18. Please indicate the *main* jobs you have held, giving the names of the
    organizations in which you were employed, the positions you held
    within the organizations, and the approximate dates. (List in order
    from "most recent" to "least recent.")
    Employing Organization   Positions Held   Dates

_____

_____

19. Please list the clubs and organizations you belong to and any respon-
    sible positions you have held in them such as committee membership
    or offices.
    Name of Organization   Positions Held

_____

_____

Continue on the back if necessary, and also note there any additional
comments or explanations you may wish to make.

II. EYOA Board of Directors, September 1965 to June 1968

(Compiled from board minutes. In last column, a number following an ampersand—as & 4—indicates number of meetings to which the members sent a substitute.)

Representative from	Name and position in agency	Dates of service	Length of service (Years/ Months)	Meetings attended/ Meetings held
United Way	Cyril Nigg, Board member	9/65 to 6/68	2/10	53/76
Coordinating Councils	Lillian Millard, President	4/67 to 6/68	1/3	23/32
	Cornish Rogers	8/66 to 3/67	8 mos.	7/16
	Bette Cook	9/65 to 7/66	11 mos.	26/28
AFL-CIO	Irvin Mazzei, President	9/65 to 6/68	2/10	62/76
Welfare Planning Council	John Andreson, Board member	12/65 to 6/68	2/7	55/67
	John Wellman	9/65 to 11/65	3 mos.	3/9
League of California Cities, ex officio	Howard Day, none	3/67 to 3/68	1/1	2/25
	Edwin Wade	9/65 to 2/67	1/6	6/43 & 4
County District 1	Albert Romo	3/66 to 3/68	2 yrs.	48/51
	Juanita Morales	4/68 to 6/68	3 mos.	6/8
County District 2	Juan Gonzalez	3/66 to 3/68	2 yrs.	27/51
	Rudy Aguilar	4/68 to 6/68	3 mos.	8/8
County District 3	Nancy Murphy	3/66 to 3/68	2 yrs.	38/51
	Dolores Shaw	4/68 to 6/68	3 mos.	6/8
County District 8	Clara Braid	7/67 to 3/68	9 mos.	17/17
	Joseph Alexander	4/68 to 6/68	3 mos.	8/8
City District 4	Theresa Barajas	3/66 to 3/68	2 yrs.	50/51
	Jesus Flores	4/68 to 6/68	3 mos.	8/8
City District 5	Ursula Gutierrez	3/66 to 6/68	2/3	53/59
City District 6	Samuel J. Anderson	3/66 to 3/68	2 yrs.	51/51
	Sarah Tarver	4/68 to 6/68	3 mos.	8/8

Representative from	Name and position in agency	Dates of service	Length of service (Years/Months)	Meetings attended/ Meetings held
City District 7	Evelyn Copeland	3/66 to 3/68	2 yrs.	47/51
	Eve Berry	4/68 to 6/68	3 mos.	8/8
Interim Community	John Serrato	9/65 to 2/66	6 mos.	17/17
Representatives	Rosita Moreno	9/65 to 2/66	6 mos.	14/17
	Othata Phillips	9/65 to 2/66	6 mos.	15/17
	Hays Sanders	9/65 to 2/66	6 mos.	15/17
	Elizabeth Jackson	9/65 to 2/66	6 mos.	16/17
	Savaletta Gordon	9/65 to 2/66	6 mos.	12/17
	Lillian Aceves	9/65 to 2/66	6 mos.	11/17
County Schools	Jack Landrum, Director of Federal Projects	9/65 to 6/68	2/10	63/76
	Robert Bock, Board member	3/67 to 6/68	1/4	18/33
	Howard Day	9/65 to 2/67	1/6	41/43
	Robert McCaughn, Assistant Superintendent	9/65 to 6/68	2/10	58/76
County	Joseph Heartz, Deputy Director, Personnel	11/67 to 6/68	8 mos.	13/16 & 2
	Ellis Murphy	9/65 to 10/67	2/2	37/60
County	Roy Hoover, Chief, Special Services, C.A.O.	10/67 to 6/68	9 mos.	13/17 & 1
	Ernest Debs	9/65 to 9/67	2/1	18/45 & 3
	Carl Terwilliger, Director, Employee Services, Probation	11/67 to 6/68	8 mos.	15/16
	Leland Carter	9/65 to 10/67	2/2	32/59 & 9
City Schools	Sam Hamerman Assistant Superintendent	9/65 to 6/68	2/10	43/76 & 14
	Josie Bain, Assistant Superintendent	9/65 to 6/68	2/10	5/76 & 6
	William Zazueta, Principal	9/65 to 6/68	2/10	49/76
City	Willard Murray, Executive Assistant to the Mayor	7/67 to 6/68	1 yr.	19/24
	E. Hawkins	4/66 to 6/67	1/6	24/32
	Billy Mills	9/65 to 3/66	7 mos.	18/20
	Alerico Ortega, Commissioner of Public Works	9/65 to 6/68	2/10	54/76 & 3
	Robert Goe, Executive Assistant to the Mayor	9/65 to 6/68	2/10	36/76 & 1

NOTES
★ ★ ★

Notes

Complete authors' names, titles, and publication data may be found in the Bibliography, pages 199–206.

CHAPTER 1

1. 78 U.S. Stat. 508, sec. 202, 3.

2. This requirement has also led to other types of participation by the poor, for example, as trainees, as members of advisory groups, and in newly created nonprofessional positions. But the participation of the poor in decision-making bodies appears to be the widest departure from tradition. See the sections on resident participation in U.S. Congress, Senate Subcommittee, *Examination of the War on Poverty, 1967.*

3. Milbrath, *Political Participation*, pp. 16–17.

4. Office of Public Information and Research Division, EYOA. The expenditures cover a two and a half year period. Between September 1965 and 1967, EYOA was responsible for all of Los Angeles County. Then early in 1967 four smaller CAAs were created within Los Angeles County: one each in Long Beach, Compton, East Los Angeles, and Pasadena.

5. The expressions "community representative" and "representative of the poor" are used as synonyms throughout this study.

6. Selznick, *TVA and the Grass Roots*, p. 264.

7. Almond and Verba, *The Civic Culture.*

8. Milbrath, *Political Participation*, p. 151. See also Almond and Verba, *The Civic Culture.* For a review of the literature on social and political participation see Marshall, "Who Participates in What: A Bibliographic Essay on Individual Participation in Urban Areas," pp. 201–224.

9. Hausknecht, "The Blue Collar Joiner." Gans, *The Urban Villagers.* Bachrach, *The Theory of Democratic Elitism.* Walker, "A Critique of the Elitist Theory of Democracy," pp. 285–295. See Greer and Orleans, "Political Sociology," pp. 814–815, for a discussion of differential access.

10. Lipset, *Political Man*, pp. 86–126.

11. Scoble, "Interdisciplinary Perspectives on Poverty in America." See also the article by Nathan Glazer in Gordon, *Poverty in America.*

12. The poverty program offers opportunities for studies with both practical and theoretical relevance for many other questions as well. For an illustration of how research oriented toward poverty policy can add to social science theory, see Jaros *et al.*, "The Malevolent Leader," pp. 564–575.

13. Milbrath, *Political Participation*, pp. 140–141.

14. Two previous studies of the effect of citizen participation which provide

the closest parallels with this analysis are Rossi and Dentler's treatment of the impact of citizen participation on urban renewal in Chicago, *The Politics of Urban Renewal*, and Selznick's study of formal and informal participation on TVA, *TVA and the Grass Roots*.

15. Relatively little work has been done in this area; see references in Brim and Wheeler, *Socialization after Childhood*.

16. Note the growing use of nonprofessionals as aides in teaching and medicine and of the poor as representatives in public and private agencies, such as area redevelopment boards, model cities, and school groups. See Mogulof, "Citizen Participation," mimeographed working paper, 1970.

17. The published material on this topic is meager. See Banfield, *Big City Politics*; Crouch and Dinerman, *Southern California Metropolis*; Blake, *You Wear the Big Shoe*; Wilson, "A Guide to Reagan Country," pp. 37–45. See also citations in Lee, *Politics of Nonpartisanship*; Abrahams, "Functioning of Boards and Commissions in the Los Angeles City Government"; and Town Hall, Los Angeles, *A Study of the Los Angeles City Charter*.

18. See Hauser and Schnore, *The Study of Urbanization*, p. 138.

19. The board included twenty-four voting members and one active nonvoting member who was chairman.

20. It is important to note that the research took place prior to three events of great significance for EYOA: the change in the executive director in 1968, the change in the national administration in 1969, and the mayoralty election in Los Angeles in 1969.

21. See Appendix I. Throughout this study board members are referred to as community representatives or agency representatives. Some board members would argue that the term "representative" is incorrectly used to describe the board members. They do not see these members primarily in the role of representatives (see chapter 4 on the conflicting notions of the role of board members) but for simplicity they are referred to as representatives.

22. Festinger and Katz, eds., *Research Methods in the Behavioral Sciences*.

23. See comments on this problem in Rossi and Dentler, *The Politics of Urban Renewal*.

24. To protect anonymity all subjects are referred to as males.

25. The decision was made not to ask permission in advance to tape the interviews, but rather to walk into the interview with a small portable cassette-style tape recorder in full view. Then, after explaining the nature of the interview, to state matter-of-factly that the interviews were all being taped just because that was easier than taking notes. No objections were voiced. This procedure was suggested by Elinson, *Folk Politics*, p. 21.

26. See Rossi and Dentler, *Politics of Urban Renewal*, p. 8, and Hunt, Crane, and Wahlke, "Interviewing Political Elites in Cross-Cultural Comparative Research," pp. 59–68, who comment on the same phenomenon.

27. Sixteen out of seventeen were returned.

28. These results are analyzed in detail in chapter 6 and provide an interesting comparison with the retrospective recall data on the learning of other board members in chapter 5.

29. See Lee, *The Politics of Nonpartisanship*, p. 45.

30. See Schwartz and Schwartz, "Problems in Participant Observation," pp. 343–353. The topic of the proper role of a participant observer deserves fuller treatment than is possible here. It seems particularly difficult in field research to separate the role of social scientist from the role of private citizen. It is difficult to overcome the urge to enter into the fray, to attempt to manipulate the subjects by suggesting ways they could accomplish their goals. Further, it is difficult to maintain a certain distance. If you have lunch with people, are in their homes, and see

their problems, you have the urge to get involved. Do you also have the responsibility or does social science absolve one of those responsibilities? One also feels qualms about writing in abstract terms about people whom one has come to know as individuals.

31. Becker and Geer provide a useful comparison of the results of field observation and unstructured interviews in "Participant Observation and Interviewing," pp. 28–32.

32. Mailer, "The Steps of the Pentagon."

33. See Yablonsky, *The Hippie Trip.* He says, "I am a social scientist who considers it almost impossible to be totally objective in the study of human behavior. There are simply too many personal and situational variables in the human condition for a student of society to become fully detached." In addition to acknowledging their own subjectivity, researchers have an obligation to make clear their own background, just as they study the backgrounds of others. This researcher can be classified as a White Anglo-Saxon Protestant upper middle class thirtyish female college graduate from a moderate Republican background. I am a liberal on civil rights and welfare issues but suffer from ambivalence because I am unable to label clearly either the establishment or the radicals and minorities as the devils of society. I am committed to the value of the American system and steeped in the viewpoint of those in the establishment about the problems of change, yet I persist in believing that the system can and must change to meet new circumstances.

34. Responses were received from approximately half the respondents.

35. For treatment of this topic see Bibby and Davidson, *On Capitol Hill*; Scoble, "Perspectives on Poverty"; Levitan, "Planning the Anti-Poverty Strategy"; Graham, "The Politics of Poverty"; Donovan, *The Politics of Poverty*; Marris and Rein, *Dilemmas of Social Reform.*

36. Donovan, *The Politics of Poverty*, p. 39. See also Scoble, "Perspectives on Poverty," p. 9.

37. 78 Stat. 508, sec. 202, 3. The U.S. Advisory Commission on Intergovernmental Relations, *Intergovernmental Relations in the Poverty Program: A Commission Report*, pp. 24–25, points out that allowing communities to administer CAAs through private agencies rather than solely through local government agencies was a divergence from the usual grant-in-aid procedures.

38. Rubin, "Maximum Feasible Participation," cites letters from various members of the Shriver task force which illustrate the lack of consensus on the origins of the idea. Moynihan describes four different interpretations of the purpose of community action and maximum feasible participation: coordination, power and conflict, service, and pragmatism. See "What is Community Action?" See also his "The Professors and the Poor."

39. Mogulof, "A Developmental Approach to the Community Action Program Idea," pp. 12–20.

40. Ferman *et al., Poverty in America*, analyzes various approaches to poverty along these dimensions. Moynihan, in *Maximum Feasible Misunderstanding*, equates the latter view with extreme conflict and attempts to use the poor to destroy the whole political system. Robert Levine in the *Washington Post*, Sunday, January 19, 1969, argues convincingly that the conflict view of community action does not necessarily entail that extreme; it can mean limited pressure not designed to overthrow the system but to gradually change institutions by means of politics.

41. U.S. Office of Economic Opportunity, Community Action Program, *Community Action Program Guide.*

42. U.S. Congress Senate Committee, *Expand the War on Poverty*, Hearings, 1965, p. 265. See also Stringfellow, "Representation of the Poor in American Society," pp. 142–151; Haddad, "Mr. Shriver and the Savage Politics of Poverty," pp. 44–45. For further analysis of why the mayors opposed the idea, see Greenstone

and Peterson, "Reformers, Machines, and the War on Poverty," a paper presented at the 1966 American Political Science Association meeting.

43. Economic Opportunity Act as amended in Sec. 202 C, and U.S. Office of Economic Opportunity, CAP memo 57, of January 11, 1967.

44. Donovan, *Politics of Poverty*, pp. 61–63, and Rubin, "Maximum Feasible Participation," p. 13; Davidson, "Creative Federalism and the War on Poverty," pp. 9–11.

45. 81 Stat. 691 sec. 210*a* and 693 sec. 211*b*. U.S. Office of Economic Opportunity, Community Action Program, *Organizing Communities for Action*, February 1968, presents guidelines for implementing the Green amendment.

46. U.S. Congress, House, *Congressional Record*, 90th Cong., 1st sess., H 16558 and H 16569, December 11, 1967. Rowland Evans and Robert Novak in the *Los Angeles Times*, October 27, 1967.

47. Yankelovich, Inc. *Study of the Effects of Sections 210 and 211 of the 1967 Amendments to the Economic Opportunity Amendments.*

48. See Rubin, "Maximum Feasible Participation"; Clark, in Senate Subcommittee, *Examination of the War on Poverty*, Hearings, 1967, pp. 292–295; Scoble, "Perspectives on Poverty," p. 16; Brager and Purcell, *Community Action against Poverty*, pp. 142–143; Rein, "Community Action Programs."

49. Rubin, "Maximum Feasible Participation," p. 14; Davidson, "Creative Federalism," p. 2.

CHAPTER 2

1. There is a growing body of data on local CAAs: Brandeis University, Florence Heller Graduate School for Advanced Studies in Social Welfare, "Board Members of Community Action Agencies: An Analysis of Interview Data," Report No. 2, August, 1968, and "Community Representation in Community Action Programs," Report No. 5, March, 1969 (Mimeographed, OEO Grant No. CG68–9499 A/2); Greenstone and Peterson, "Reformers, Machines, and the War on Poverty," and Peterson, "Forms of Representation," compare New York, Chicago, Los Angeles, and Philadelphia; another source of comparative data is in the Senate subcommittee report, *Examination of the War on Poverty*, 1967; see also Kramer's *Participation of the Poor* on CAAs in the San Francisco area; Bachrach and Baratz, *Power and Poverty*, on Baltimore.

2. See Banfield, *Political Influence*, for the distinction between formal and informal. See descriptions of Los Angeles politics in Banfield, ed, *City Politics*, p. 26. Scoble, "Negro Politics in Los Angeles: The Quest for Power." See also references cited in chapter 1, n. 17, above.

3. Greenstone and Peterson, "Reformers, Machines, and the War on Poverty," p. 9.

4. *Ibid.*, p. 14. See also Wilson, *The Amateur Democrat*, p. 104; and Sears, "Political Attitudes of Los Angeles Negroes," p. 5, on the unresponsiveness of Los Angeles political institutions to minorities.

5. Bollens, "Youth Opportunities Board of Greater Los Angeles." For an interesting history of a parallel agency see Thernstrom, *Poverty, Planning, and Politics in New Boston.*

6. Holton had originally intended for private agencies to be represented, but after Goe's joint powers proposal was agreed to, this idea was dropped. Supervisor Ernest Debs suggested that private agencies could be added later after the legal ramifications were worked out, but this was not done.

7. Marris and Rein, *Dilemmas of Social Reform*, pp. 154–157.

8. See minutes of YOB and Economic Opportunity Federation at EYOA. It is important to note that the private agencies were mainly established civic and charitable associations; most were closely linked with governmental operations.

They were the League of California Cities, the Los Angeles County Federation of Coordinating Councils, United Way, the Welfare Planning Council, the Chamber of Commerce, and the AFL-CIO. These same agencies later gained representation on EYOA.

9. Details of the creation of EYOA and the preceding conflict between YOB and EOF are discussed in Carney and Reuss, "The Politics of the War on Poverty in Los Angeles." Also see the *Los Angeles Times*, March 14, May 9 and 28, and June 8, 1965.

10. The agreement worked out by Collins was widely viewed as a victory for Mayor Yorty. See *New Republic*, September 4, 1965, "When the Poor Are Powerless," p. 7.

11. *Intergovernmental Relations in the Poverty Program*, p. 28, reports that in 1956 only 20.6 percent of the CAAs were governmental agencies. No figures were available on what percentage of the governmental agencies were intergovernmental, but the percentage would be quite low. U.S. Congress, Senate, *Congressional Record*, 90th Congress, 1st sess., S18255, December 8, 1967. Javits gives different figures in 1967—only 41 out of 1,050 CAAs, or about 4 percent, are public bodies.

12. The Chamber informed EYOA in 1965 that it would not send a representative since EYOA's programs were not within the Chamber's realm of interest.

13. The bulk of the research for the present study was done before the Green amendment changes were made, so unless otherwise specified, references to board members refer to board members prior to these changes. Additional changes in 1968 were to specify terms for agency representatives and increase community representatives' terms to three years.

14. The 1967 amendments set an upper limit of fifty-one for sizes of boards. See Senate Subcommittee, *Examination of the War on Poverty, 1967*, parts IV–VII.

15. *Ibid.* Greenstone and Peterson, "Reformers, Machines, and the War on Poverty." Prior to the 1966 requirements that a third of the board membership be poverty representatives, some boards such as Chicago had a smaller percentage of poverty representatives than Los Angeles. See *Intergovernmental Relations in the Poverty Program*, pp. 48–54.

16. Senate Subcommittee, *Examination of the War on Poverty, 1967*, parts IV–VII.

17. *Ibid.*

18. See *Los Angeles Times*, August 23, 1968, Jack Jones, "Poverty War Director Assesses Four and One-Half Year Fight."

19. *Intergovernmental Relations in the Poverty Program*, p. 45.

20. Senate Subcommittee, *Examination of the War on Poverty*, 1967, III, 798; IV, 902.

21. Rossi and Dentler, *Politics of Urban Renewal*, pp. 75, 76, and 99. The first executive director of EYOA frequently stated that maximum feasible participation does not mean merely involving poor people; it also means involving the public and private agencies. *Los Angeles Times*, August 23, 1968. Graham, "Poverty and the Legislative Process," describes how community action in Alinsky's terms meant action by the poor, but when community action was adopted by the government, community meant the local government apparatus plus influential civic and business leaders. See pp. 265–266.

22. *Intergovernmental Relations in the Poverty Program*, p. 911.

23. Chapter V in *Modern Organizations*, by Etizioni, summarizes Weber's treatment of rational bureaucracies. See also Downs, *Inside Bureaucracy*, pp. 18–19, and Mogulof, "A Developmental Approach to the Community Action Idea."

24. Critics point out that the de-emphasis of research was not inevitable. They suggest that the leadership of EYOA was not interested in research because it

involved evaluating the effectiveness of programs and a concern with conceptualization which was alien to the leadership.

25. See similar comments that OEO is increasingly being ignored. Moynihan, "Professors and the Poor," p. 19.

26. Senate Subcommittee, *Examination of the War on Poverty, 1967.*

27. *Los Angeles Times*, August 23, 1968. Since his resignation the tenure of executive directors is decreasing (his successor lasted for one year) and infighting about the position is increasing.

28. Greenstone and Peterson, "Reformers, Machines, and the War on Poverty," p. 9.

29. See Senate subcommittee, *Examination of the War on Poverty, 1967*, IV, 906. U.S. Office of Economic Opportunity, *Organizing Communities for Action*, p. 13. For further comparisons of election systems, see the American Arbitration Association, "Study of CAP Elections." Greenstone and Peterson, "Reformers, Machines, and the War on Poverty," pp. 9, 10.

30. U.S. Office of Economic Opportunity, *Organizing Communities for Action*, pp. 12, 13.

31. At the September 13, 1965, board meeting, a motion (made by City Councilman Mills and seconded by Goe, the Mayor's executive assistant) stated that nominees and voters in the election must have family incomes of $4,000 per year or less. The $4,000 figure reflects an early OEO regulation that to be a recipient of a community action program, a family's income must be not more than $4,000. This regulation paralleled Keyserling's definition of poverty as a family income under $4,000 a year. (Keyserling, *Poverty and Deprivation in the United States.*) Later studies recommended using a flexible criteria of poverty, taking into account differences in family size, regional standards of living, and so forth.

32. Using this figure it could be argued that since 47 percent of the poor are concentrated in poverty areas (where at least 25 percent of the families are at the poverty level) the election should be directed at these communities the way the actual programs are. The Research Division of EYOA, however, does not currently have information available to support these figures. Table I in "Poverty Areas in Los Angeles County" by Meeker and Street indicates that an even smaller percentage of the poor live in the ten identified poverty areas.

33. These people also point out that the large districts would make it harder for congressmen to get control of the elections. Lack of concern for the power base of the representatives is shown by the fact that staff members did not see the voting districts as representative districts but merely as units of convenience for the election process (memo from Lloyd Street to Joe Maldonado, January 10, 1966).

34. Study reveals that the inequities in the districts were primarily the result of careless work by EYOA staff members responsible for setting the boundaries. See Marshall, "War Over Poverty: Politics of the Los Angeles Poverty Election."

35. At 57 of the 156 polling places no ballots were cast.

36. Other figures quoted in *Yale Law Journal*, "Participation of the Poor," p. 618: 4.2 percent in Cleveland and 5.3 percent in Kansas City. Comparison of percentage of turnout is dangerous since estimates of the number of eligible voters vary so much. In Los Angeles, estimates varied from 300,000 to 1 million.

37. Comparison of the number of candidates in the election of community representatives:

District	1st election	2d election	District	1st election	2d election
I	5	3	V	10	4
II	11	2	VI	13	9
III	4	3	VII	6	8
IV	7	5	VIII	0	2

Total: first election, 56; second election, 36.

38. There are no turnout figures by income in traditional elections but some indications are provided by the following figures: (1) Political Behavior Archives, University of California, Los Angeles, data from three of the fourteen areas of Los Angeles County with highest concentration of Negroes, showed that in 1960, 69 percent of eligible registered, 82 percent of registered voted, thus 56 percent of eligible voted; (2) Political Behavior Archives, UCLA, data from a sample census tract with median income below $4,000 showed that 28 percent of those eligible voted in 1962.

39. American Arbitration Association, "Study of CAP Elections," pp. 9, 11, cites school district elections in suburban New York, where 4.4 percent of registrants vote and only 2.5 percent of eligibles vote. Lee, *Politics of Nonpartisanship*, cites variation in turnouts for local elections, ranging from 15 percent to 71 percent (p. 138.) Los Angeles is noted for the lack of local citizen participation in politics; Wilson, *Amateur Democrat*, pp. 96–125. Los Angeles residents with at least some college education participate less in local political affairs (and are less socially active informally and in voluntary associations) than in the rest of the United States; Bayes, "Political Participation and Geographic Mobility in Los Angeles County."

40. American Arbitration Association, "Study of CAP Elections," p. 10. The description of the election of the Los Angeles County Central Democratic Committee as a hopeless lottery could easily be applied to the poverty elections; Wilson, *Amateur Democrat*, p. 99.

41. Lee, *Politics of Nonpartisanship*, p. 120.

42. *Ibid.*, p. 122. Ostrum in "School Board Politics: An Analysis of Non-Partisanship in the Los Angeles City Board of Education," points out that this obscurity occurs in nonpartisan school board elections. See chapter 3 for more details of the election campaigns.

43. *Yale Law Journal,*"Participation of the Poor," p. 618. Kramer in *Participation of the Poor*, p. 197, reports similar findings in the San Francisco area.

44. Greenstone and Peterson, "Reformers, Machines, and the War on Poverty," pp. 9–10. Peterson, in "Forms of Representation," points out that direct election enabled mayors to avoid that charges they were dominating the boards while still preventing hostile organizations from getting control.

45. Lee, *Politics of Nonpartisanship*, p. 159, sets forth criteria for both the competition and consensus which are essential to the democratic process.

CHAPTER 3

1. Appendix II gives the names and positions of board members and their length of service.

2. EYOA personnel estimate the EYOA staff changes as much as a third every year. All the original department heads have left EYOA and the executive director was one of the few CAA directors who kept his job for almost three years.

3. Brandeis University, "Board Members of Community Action Agencies," p. 6.

4. Chapter 2 describes the Joint Powers Agreement.

5. A Negro city councilman was originally on the board but he was replaced by a Negro commissioner of public works. The councilman was replaced soon after a controversial vote in which he was the only agency representative to vote with all the community representatives. All agree that the replacement was a political change. Some explain that the mayor did not want to have a representative who voted this way. Others say that the councilman wanted to drop off because EYOA was a political liability, forcing him to take positions that might be unpopular. See Crain *et al.*, *The Politics of School Desegregation*, p. 178, for comments on the

plight of elected politicians on boards. The Negro commissioner was later replaced by a Negro member of the mayor's staff on the grounds that the commissioner did not have time for the job. But the Mexican-American representative who had been on the mayor's staff did not resign from EYOA when he became commissioner of public works. The Board of Public Works is the only full-time board in the Los Angeles city government. See Town Hall, Los Angeles, *Study of the Los Angeles City Charter*, p. 157.

6. In 1965 public assistance was technically a bureau, but later it achieved full departmental status after a series of organizational modifications.

7. The resignation of the county supervisor is attributed to a lack of time but one can speculate that it also represented a lack of desire to continue on the board, owing to a feeling that the board's activities had become routinized. There is also evidence that the chief administrative officer (CAO) was dissatisfied with the total county team because they were not giving strong enough support to the county's interests (see Crouch, *Southern California Metropolis*, p. 187, on the authority of the CAO's office). The supervisor was replaced by the chief of the Special Services Division of the CAO's office, whose job involves intergovernmental relations. The head of public assistance was replaced by a man from the personnel department, a central staff department that ostensibly has a larger picture than public assistance and would not be oriented to only one department. The head of probation was replaced by a subordinate in his department, but the trend toward domination by staff departments was completed with the July 1968 restructuring of the board when the county dropped the representative of the Probation Department.

8. The original county board of education member resigned from that job when he was appointed to the State Board of Education and the county schools sent another member from its board to EYOA. But the original member remained in EYOA by being designated as a representative of the League of California Cities (in which he had not been active since he had never been an elected city official).

9. The coordinating councils send the president of the Federation of Community Coordinating Councils; the Los Angeles AFL-CIO sends its president.

10. The exception is the second League of California Cities representative (see n. 8 above) who had not been active in the league but was chairman of EYOA. The League's first representative had attended only six out of forty-three EYOA board meetings.

11. Scheslinger, *Ambition and Politics*, stresses the impact of career aspirations on the behavior of public officials.

12. Some staff members resent the fact that agencies are increasingly picking lower level employees to sit on the board.

13. See chapter 4.

14. The first group of elected community representatives are also referred to throughout this report as the original or old community representatives. The second group of elected representatives are also called the new community representatives. The one representative who was reelected will be included in the old group in this section on recruitment.

15. Some staff members felt independent militant organizations might put up candidates in the second election, but they did not. One potential candidate never turned in a petition, and another one turned in a petition that was disqualified because the signatures were not from the candidate's district. The ruling was not contested.

16. The most blatant example of manipulation was the decision to have a candidate from a Veterans' Administration facility so that that district would show a large vote which would actually consist almost entirely of residents of the facility.

17. One of the original community representatives and one of the new ones

specifically mentioned that the poverty organization they took the initiative to contact was just a few doors away from where they lived.

18. Evidence of the importance of being personally asked to participate is presented in Bowman and Boynton, "Recruitment Patterns among Local Party Officials," pp. 667–676.

19. One was a senior citizen group which in return for a $10 membership fee supplied a candidate with 600 throwaway pamphlets. The other group was a civic improvement league that helped a candidate with publicity even though he did not belong to the group.

20. Prior to the second election, EYOA's election committee, composed of all the original community representatives, debated whether rules should be set to regulate campaign expenditures. But after touching on many of the issues raised by legislators concerned with governmental election rules, the committee gave up because they could not agree on what types of help were fair and could not provide for the enforcement of rules. This result should seem familiar to those who have tried to regulate campaigns.

21. Lee, *Politics of Nonpartisanship*, pp. 120, 122. Tallies from certain Head Start sites showed they voted overwhelmingly for candidates connected with the local group.

22. Two because their area was no longer part of EYOA's area, and two because their family was over the $4,000 limit.

23. The community representatives made the decision to have "incumbent" listed after their names on the ballot.

24. See citations in Kain and Ries, Congressmen, Incumbency, and the Elections."

25. See table 2 in chapter 2. This losing incumbent feels that he would have won if there had not been a mix-up in getting ballots to one of the sites where he had a lot of support. This mix-up was the topic of a protest to the election committee but it was disallowed, because the committee felt EYOA had not been at fault.

26. See Matthews, *U.S. Senators*, and Wahlke and Eulau *et al.*, *The Lesislative System*; Warner *et al.*, *The American Federal Executive*; Huckshorn, "Spotlight on City Councilmen."

27. The Brandeis University study includes socioeconomic data on board members but it has not included the largest metropolitan areas in its sample. Two studies of poverty board candidates also provide data relevant to community representatives on boards: White, "Articulateness, Political Mobility, and Conservatism"; and Bowen and Massotti, "Spokesmen for the Poor," pp. 89–100.

28. In the discussion of socioeconomic characteristics, the reelected community representative is included in both the old and the new groups.

29. Brandeis University, "Board Members of Community Action Agencies," also found that poverty representatives tend to be younger than other board members.

30. The prevalence of women on this board suggests important questions about the nature of the war on poverty. Is it a woman's activity, similar to church? See Moynihan, "Professors and the Poor," p. 23, for an affirmative answer. Or does this simply reflect matriarchical segments of lower class life? Brandeis University, "Board Members of Community Action Agencies," found that poverty representatives on about half the boards included a majority of women.

31. Brandeis University, "Board Members of Community Action Agencies," presents similar results.

32. The other representatives in each case were Caucasians—one elected from a district with a large proportion of both Negroes and Mexican-Americans, the others from districts with a large proportion of Caucasians, many elderly.

33. Three community representatives indicated that they were brought up as

Catholics but are not Catholics now. There are two Catholics on the board who are not Mexican-Americans.

34. Two of these representatives were elected less than three years after arriving in Los Angeles.

35. Matthews, *U.S. Senators*, pp. 17–21, discusses the limitations of this indicator and describes the occupational class categories followed here.

36. Two community representatives had fathers who technically fall in the professional category, one an elected county sheriff in rural Texas, and one a minister who did a wide variety of odd jobs in order to support his family. Since both these fathers were members of minority groups it seems doubtful that the general occupational categories apply correctly to them or that there was actually downward mobility on the part of their offspring.

37. Three of the agency representatives who had parents in this category explained that their parents were immigrants to this country, two from Europe, one from Mexico, and formal schooling may not accurately reflect their level of education. Two community representatives said their parents came from Mexico; one had parents from Lebanon, and one from Europe.

38. The income of the public agency representatives falls between $16,000 and $30,000 (two did not respond to the income questions, and one said his income was below $16,000). The private agency representatives fall in noticeably higher income levels. Subjects indicated a reluctance to indicate outside sources of income in addition to salaries, and one person indicated he would answer but would not tell the truth, so the results may be unreliable.

39. Note the absence of lawyers. See comments on the prevalence of lawyers in legislatures in Matthews, *U.S. Senators*, and Wahlke and Eulau, *The Legislative System*.

40. The exception was a proprietor, but so was his family. Note that some did move from laborer to clerical jobs.

41. He dropped out after the eighth grade to help support his family.

42. Brandeis University, "Board Members of Community Action Agencies," indicates a wide variety in the educational level of community representations in the fifteen cities studied. But in two-thirds of the cities between 25 and 50 percent of the representatives did have some education beyond high school. So the Los Angeles community representatives do not have a uniquely high educational level.

43. The exceptions were two who did not respond and one who described himself as upper.

44. The exception was one who said that in his life he had been many classes, including upper middle, middle, working, and low.

45. The one exception went to the University of Maryland.

46. Eleven out of twelve of the agency representatives had staff jobs and dealt with boards or councils that have varying degrees of control over the staffs. Yet when these representatives are on EYOA, they switch roles and become board members. It is interesting to speculate on whether the board members who are most suspicious that the EYOA staff is manipulating the board are members who are most manipulative of the boards in their own agencies (see chapter 5, attitudes toward staff).

47. Four did mention the possibility of some changes in the organization they worked for. But a more typical comment was that there would be no change in the organization they worked for because "I made my decision long ago." This type of stability leads one to question the current cliché about the great geographical and organizational mobility of the college-educated population. Certainly it is a reminder that certain segments of the college-educated population are not at all open to such mobility (some might say that this example merely shows the appeal of the

Southern California climate, but it seems more likely that similar segments of the population can be found in urban centers throughout the country).

48. See chapter 5 for a discussion of the jobs they actually did get after being on the board.

49. See Miller, "The American Lower Classes: A Typological Approach," in *New Perspectives on Poverty*, Shostak and Gomberg, eds. Of course there are individual community representatives who exhibit as much family stability as the agency representatives.

50. Bowen and Massotti, in "Spokesmen for the Poor," report similar findings among the Cleveland poverty candidates.

51. Only one new community representative owns his own home, and only three of the original community representatives own their homes.

52. The term is from Matthews, *U.S. Senators*, p. 43.

53. See William Evan's critique of the organization participation scale, "Dimensions of Participation in Voluntary Associations," pp. 148–153. The situation of the public agency representatives aptly indicates the inadequacy of the typical social science index of participation, organizational membership. Many of the public representatives' jobs involve constant contact with community organizations. They would be widely acknowledged to be active participators in the community, yet some list membership in only one or two organizations which would not be interpreted as high participation. The index does not reflect accurately their high level of participation.

54. This finding must be stated cautiously because it involves comparing two different types of responses. Agency representatives were asked to describe their parents' activity in community affairs when the respondents were growing up as either very prominent, quite active, somewhat active, or hardly active. Yet the agency representatives were not asked to describe their own level of activity in these terms. Instead, they were asked merely to list the organizations to which they belonged. But it is assumed that the respondents would agree that they all would rank in the first three categories.

55. Parents' activity in community affairs and interest in politics was taken to be the most active category checked, whether it was checked for the mother or father or both. The agency representatives were also asked to describe the degree of interest their parents had in politics when they were growing up. The agency representatives were not asked to describe their own level of interest but owing to their involvement with or in governmental agencies in upper positions, one can safely assume they are all at least somewhat interested in politics, and probably very interested, as was indicated by the facility with which they referred to their political loyalties in the interviews. And three mentioned being active in campaigns. Comparing their parents' interests and their own interests, one does not find any marked increase. Thirteen of the agency representatives said their parents were somewhat interested and only three said they were hardly interested.

56. All the original community representatives belonged to two or fewer organizations (five said two, one said one, and two said none). Four of the new representatives said they belonged to at least three organizations and only four said two or fewer (two said one).

57. "Articulateness, Political Mobility, and Conservatism," White's study of the poverty candidates in Philadelphia, reports similar findings, p. 3. So do Bowen and Masotti, "Spokesmen for the Poor."

58. Chapters 5 and 6 describe changes in their activity after they had been on the board.

59. See Hughes, *Men and Their Work*.

60. See Banfield and Wilson, *City Politics*, Part IV.

61. See Matthews, *U.S. Senators*, p. 58.

62. See Meyerson and Banfield, *Politics, Planning, and the Public Interest*, p. 47.

63. Kahn *et al.*, *Organizational Stress: Studies in Role Conflict and Ambiguity*, pp. 135, 381.

64. *Ibid.*, p. 382.

65. Riessman, *Mental Health of the Poor*, p. 115.

66. Miller, "The American Lower Classes: A Typological Approach."

67. One representative is so deviant that he does not fit into any of these categories.

68. Cohen, "Los Angeles Riot Study: Summary and Implications for Policy," cites the 1965 Census of the curfew area, which shows the median income for 1964 was $4,669. Yet even using income as the criteria, there are large differences in the actual poverty of the community representatives. Compare the situation of a single man who has in the past made much more than $4,000 a year and now has his room and medical bills covered by compensation, and a divorced woman who has never made more than $4,000 and has five children and no steady work.

69. See Miller, "The American Lower Classes: A Typological Approach." See article by Linda Matthews in the *Los Angeles Times*, September 9, 1968. Also, Riessman and Glazer, *Faces in the Crowd*.

CHAPTER 4

1. For references to small group literature, see Olmsted, *The Small Group*, and Hare, "Interpersonal Relations in Small Groups," in Faris, *Handbook of Modern Sociology*. Small group studies have limited usefulness for research on a group operating as a policy-making body in a political setting since the external forces are so important.

2. No distinction is made between power and influence. Both terms are used in this chapter to mean the ability of men to realize their own will even when others resist. See Max Weber's definition in Gerth and Mills, eds., *From Max Weber: Essays in Sociology*.

3. Marris and Rein, *Dilemmas of Social Reform*, p. 168.

4. Selznick, *TVA and the Grass Roots*, p. 264.

5. Wahlke and Eulau *et al.*, *The Legislative System*, chap. 12. A trustee is seen as a free agent; a delegate follows the mandate from his constituency.

6. Brandeis University, "Board Members of Community Action Agencies," reports similar findings, pp. 9, 10.

7. Several of the private agencies they represent are confederations of voluntary agencies.

8. But he did admit that when his own agency's proposals came up he watched to be sure they did not get cut out.

9. The one exception was a lay member who said that since he was not on the payroll he did not have to check first with the agency or think of the political aspects.

10. If one accepts their comments, they seem to be well socialized into accepting the views of their agencies. Birth control was the one major issue of conflict mentioned.

11. Note the perception gap between this picture of being very responsive and the feeling of community representatives that the agencies and EYOA are not responsive to the community (see chapter 5, below).

12. In this chapter and chapter 5, the term "community representative" refers solely to the original group of elected community representatives. If the new community representatives are mentioned, they are referred to by that title. The per-

ceptions of the new community representatives about the functioning of the board are treated in chapter 6.

13. Brandeis University, "Board Members of Community Action Agencies," pp. 10–11, also found that community representatives saw themselves as representing a particular constituency. But their index does not distinguish between those who saw their constituency as a district and those who saw it as an organization.

14. Using Wahlke and Eulau's two types of areal roles (chapter 13), district and state orientation, most of the representatives had district orientation.

15. Scoble, "Negro Politics," p. 15, stresses the almost paranoiac fear among Negroes of being "sold out." Sears, in "Political Attitudes of Los Angeles Negroes," did not find this distrust but it seems to be operating in the EYOA community representatives. Yet agency representatives also expressed great distrust of other agency representatives. See chapter 3, and pp. 58–59.

16. The community representative who was the most certain that others were put up by organizations, and who stressed himself as a loner, was the only one who specifically mentioned getting campaign help from an organization.

17. Some executive staff people felt that community representatives were just looking for excuses for not doing the job they could have done without help.

18. Both city councilmen and county supervisors work full time and have field staffs. The poverty representatives' districts are similar in area to the supervisorial districts, yet the community representatives work only part time and have much less assistance than the supervisors.

19. When community representatives ask at board meetings how to handle complaints from specific organizations, they are told to refer them to the executive director and not to become personally involved.

20. One representative moved out of the district to escape the criticism.

21. Gross, Mason, and McEachern, *Explorations in Role Analysis: Studies of the School Superintendency Role,* p. 321, describes various ways in which expectations (or roles) are learned. One is when neither the position incumbent or the counterposition incumbent has clear expectations and they are worked out by trial and error. This description comes closest to fitting the board situation.

22. See EYOA publication, "The Board and the Administration—Their Roles, Expectations, and Relationships" (mimeographed). The position taken is that all board members are responsible to serve the poor throughout the county, not "special interest groups."

23. Note that when the Green amendment created openings on the board for new private organizations, one of the rationales for not picking a Negro and a Mexican-American organization was that the Negroes and Mexican-Americans were already represented. But this avoided the issue that no Negro or Mexican-American *organizations* were explicitly represented—if any of the community representatives try to represent such groups they are criticized for representing special interests.

24. See Wilson, ed., *City Politics and Public Policy.* Wilson points out the different labels applied to a unitary conception of the public good by Williams and Adrian, Agger and Goldrich, Robert Wood, Banfield, and Wilson.

25. When the election committee made up of all the community representatives had a chance to change the election system for the second election, they rejected the idea of permitting existing community organizations to be involved. They reasoned, like the joint powers, that this would open the door to control by powerful groups.

26. Even the question of what the key decisions had been did not seem to have much meaning to many of the respondents. So the responses are incomplete, coming mainly from members who had been on the board a long time and who had thought in these terms.

27. This dependency suggests the need for more research on the changes in relative power taking place among governmental levels. See Scheiber, "The Con-

dition of American Federalism: An Historian's View," in a report prepared for the Senate Subcommittee on Intergovernmental Relations.

28. Any attempt to measure the controversial issues raises the question of what indicators will be used. The minutes of the EYOA Board do not record all votes taken on an issue, often only the vote that resolved the issue is given. And at times the minutes will fail to indicate negative votes on a given issue. Further, sometimes an issue that comes before the board is broken down into several parts and several votes taken but at other times the issue is voted on as a whole. The amount of subdividing does not relate to the level of controversy. The number of votes taken was arrived at by using the votes recorded in the minutes as a base, then eliminating routine votes, those that *never* received any negative votes—for example, on minutes, out of county travel, commendations for retiring members, and authorization for signatures on official transactions. The reasoning was to avoid biasing the results unduly in the direction that would show unanimity. In addition votes that were not in the minutes but which were clearly indicated by my notes were added if these votes were not unanimous.

29. Interim representatives were appointed by the city and county to serve from September 1965 until March 1966, when the election was held for the first group of community representatives.

30. The only election issue of controversy was whether the candidates would be required to have a family income of less than $4,000. When one of the interim community representatives raised the issue, the $4,000 criteria was upheld by a 14 to 6 vote.

31. Just as the agency representatives were vague on key issues, their remarks were inconclusive about splits among agency representatives. They did, however, present a clearer picture of factions among the community representatives.

32. Only two public agency representatives forthrightly agreed that there is bloc voting. One explained: "We decided . . . in the establishment's interest we ought to try to build a bloc that we could use when we had to but it would be smart not to make this too obvious. If you want to get along with the community representatives you have got to break down this 'we and they' sort of thing. So we decided we would deliberately split up and quarrel with one another over things that didn't count." This attempt to avoid the appearance of voting together may help explain the lack of awareness among other board members of blocs.

33. And public agency representatives agree to the extent of saying that their agencies are in EYOA at least partly for the monetary, public relations, and power rewards that can result for their agencies. For example, the schools see it as a chance to get money for innovations and to show the community that they do not have horns. The city is in it for the money and for the chance to get more influence in dealing with social problems (see Marris and Rein, *Dilemmas of Social Reform,* pp. 154, 155). While the private agency and community representatives see this motivation as sinister, the public agency representatives do not, partly because they are assuming that what is good for their agency is good for the community as a whole, and the poverty community in particular.

34. See chapter 3.

35. See p. 53; also Rossi and Dentler, *Politics of Urban Renewal,* on the distrust among groups involved in urban renewal, p. 111.

36. For example, see *Los Angeles Times,* May 8, 1967, which states that the County Board of Education supports county positions on the war on poverty.

37. Some educators on the board feel that the bureaucrats are more political than the politicians.

38. Four agency representatives said that at first there was a community representative bloc but that now these representatives are split on almost every issue. Some of the private agency representatives talked in general terms about the com-

munity voting one way and the establishment voting another, but when commenting more specifically on a community bloc agreed that the community split. This suggests that they saw some of the community representatives as consistently opposed to the establishment even though not all the community representatives were.

39. This parallels the division among the agency representatives on the question.

40. The Jones case caused more public uproar than any other issue in EYOA's history prior to 1969. Mrs. Jones was fired for insubordination by Joe Maldonado in the spring of 1966. Against the objections of the community representatives the board supported the director's action. But in this case the angry protests of Mrs. Jones's supporters in the community, including Congressman Hawkins, helped convince the director to reverse his action and to rehire Mrs. Jones in a complicated compromise designed to quiet the controversy. The board then supported his action.

41. The Brown Act of 1953 requires that public business be conducted at open meetings and forbids secret sessions that exclude the press and public.

42. See the attendance record of individual board members in Appndix II. An analysis of the attendance patterns at board meetings shows that between January and June of 1968 the average number of members present was eighteen out of twenty-five. That means that seven members (or approximately a third of the board) were absent at the average meeting.

43. Negative is used to mean both "no" votes and abstentions, because since thirteen votes are needed to pass a measure those who abstain are in effect helping to defeat the measure. Four or more votes are used as the indicator of very controversial issues since initial analysis of votes with three or more showed similar patterns to those with four or more and using five or more as the cut-off made the number too small.

44. Contrast this with the report that in Philadelphia the twelve poor representatives often vote together as a whole group and can get a majority of fifteen votes when they win three others. Shostak, "Promoting Participation for the Poor," pp. 64–72.

45. When the board chairman resigned in March 1968 county and community representatives allied to help elect a board chairman they felt would not be in the executive director's pocket.

46. An analysis of the minutes prior to January 1968 shows twelve issues on which there were four or more negative votes and reveals one major difference in the blocs. The community representatives are the only ones who are recorded as voting against the rest of the board. There were occasions when one or two agency representatives vote with community representatives against the rest, but there is nothing comparable with the county bloc.

47. Only once in twelve meetings did one of the joint powers fail to send any representatives.

48. County, seven times; county schools, twice; city, once; city schools, never.

49. For examples of studies primarily concerned with the culture of a political group, see Fenno, "The Appropriations Committee as a Political System," in Peabody and Polsby, eds., *New Perspectives on the House of Representatives*, and Manley, "The House Committee on Ways and Means," pp. 927–939.

50. Whether this is evidence of occupational socialization or self-selection, the difference in perspective is striking. Various types of members define the game differently and have different conceptions of what is proper and improper participation, conceptions linked with their assumptions about the representational roles described above.

51. The data must be interpreted cautiously because some respondents seemed to list people they listened to themselves and some mentioned names they thought others listened to even if they themselves did not.

52. There was no limit on the number of influential members a respondent

could list. Most mentioned three to five names. Mutual choices were not prevalent.

53. The community representatives' comments on influential agency representatives paralleled to a degree the comments of the agency representatives, which are the only ones tabulated here.

54. Negative mentions are when a respondent says "x, no he's not influential."

55. See chapter 2; as pointed out in chapter 1 the stress on coordination involves a consensus and a paternalistic mode of change.

56. See Killian's study of the ineffectiveness of Negroes on integrated committees which stress cooperation. Killian and Grigg, *Racial Crisis in America: Leadership in Conflict.* John Gardner, Chairman of the National Urban Coalition, said that the only good urban coalitions are those generating controversy because they at least are confronting the problems honestly. *Los Angeles Times,* September 13, 1968. Political scientists need to give attention to specifying the conditions in which conflict is harmful, however, as well as to those in which it is productive.

57. The reference throughout is to the first executive director of EYOA.

58. See EYOA mimeograph "The Board and the Administration—Their Roles, and Expectations, and Relationship." This memorandum stressed that the board must not interfere with the executive director's relationship with his staff and must deal with the staff only through the executive director. Interviws with the executive director showed that he felt both community representatives and agency representatives did attempt to interfere too much.

59. EYOA has 300 employees on the staff. Half of these are professionals, many with social work backgrounds.

60. Chapter 5 discusses board members' attitudes toward the staff.

61. The clearest example is the vote on Neighborhood Youth Corps; the joint powers representatives who voted for the EYOA staff recommendations apparently did not agree with them but felt it was not worth fighting the director about them.

62. See chapter 1.

63. For example, Goe, for the city, Supervisor Debs for the county, and Superintendent Crowther of the city schools.

64. Note that the original proposed changes were not referred to committee.

65. Note that when an ad hoc committee was set up to decide on the Neighborhood Youth Corps, an issue about which the agencies were very concerned, only two of the seven members were community representatives.

66. There is disagreement over whether the staff originally thought of the NAM or whether community representatives made the suggestion to the staff. Community representatives are reported to have felt they could represent the Mexican-American and Negro groups adequately and that NAM might be able to provide material assistance to EYOA.

67. The agency representatives indicated privately that regardless of their own feelings about the desirability of having the NAM on the board, they did not want to vote against any minority group. See section above on representation.

68. And no one asked which of the private interests listed in Green were represented by the League of California Cities or why, if the League represented public groups, it was not substituted for one of the eight public agencies to avoid having the present total of nine representatives of public groups (more than a third of the board).

69. When a board member suggested rotating the NAM and Chamber, no one followed up the idea.

70. The frequent reversals individuals made in their positions is evidence of lack of previous thought about board issues.

71. This pattern is classical. Many different works testify to the predominance of paid staff in organizations. On the "iron law of oligarchy" see Michels, *Political Parties,* p. 401, and Lipset *et al., Union Democracy,* pp. 1–16. See also the literature

on city managers, such as Kammerer *et al.*, *City Managers in Politics*, and the literature on school boards, such as Gross, Mason, and McEachern, *Explorations in Role Analysis: Studies of the School Superintendency.*

72. See Braybrooke and Lindblom, *A Strategy of Decision: Policy Evaluation as a Social Process*, chapters 4 and 5, which stresses prevalence and value of disjointed incremental decision-making. See Freeman and Sherwood, "Research in Large-Scale Intervention Programs," pp. 11–28, for a contrasting view.

73. One explanation is that agency representatives originally attended more often than community representatives but when the latter started receiving per diem payments for attendance, they came regularly. The result was that committee meetings got longer and the agency representatives, feeling they were too time-consuming, stopped coming.

74. When two or more informed agency representatives attended committee meetings they made a noticeable contribution to the conduct of the meeting. Their experience in meetings showed in their ability to summarize issues which community representatives raised and to search for proposals which would be acceptable to all present. They also served as a needed counterbalance to the staff.

75. The committees are often used by factions of the staff to bolster their position in a conflict.

76. This description of the way in which the executive director and the staff avoided controversy views the relationship between the director and the board members from only one direction—that of the board members. One conclusion is that the director is a key influence on the operation of the board. This is accurate. It would not be accurate, however, to conclude that he always gets his way with the board. If one looks at the relations between the director and the board from the point of view of the director, numerous examples could be given of times when the board frustrated his plans. An exchange that illustrates how the relationship looks to the director occurred when a community representative said with a smile that the board is *supposed* to boss the director. The director quickly looked up and said there wasn't any question in his mind that the board *was actually* bossing him. And the staff was often very frank in saying that they thought the board ruins proposals made by the staff by changing them to fit the interests they represent. Thus board meetings did not simply give ritual approval to the staff positions. The meetings did keep open the possibility of checking the staff and this possibility must have an effect on the way the staff worked (see Abrahams, "Functioning of Boards and Commissions," pp. 277–278).

77. For example, on EYOA personnel matters, selection of new groups for the board, or elections. Between January and June there was only one case in which committee members succeeded in passing the responsibility back to the director.

78. Talk of influence, manipulation, and control is not meant to have a negative connotation. From many perspectives they are very desirable and EYOA could not function in the same way if the staff did not have a strong influence on the board. Proof of this is provided by the increase in controversies that occurred in board meetings once the executive director resigned. Many conflicts of interests among the agencies which had previously been handled by the executive director (and prior to March 1968, by the board chairman with a cooperative as opposed to a fighting style) came out into the open. Furthermore, it is interesting that the arrival of the new executive director in November 1968 reopened many conflicts for power which had been tacitly settled by Maldonado.

79. See chapter 5 for more details on the representatives' attitudes toward EYOA and for the existence of some dissatisfaction.

80. Brandeis University, "Board Members of Community Action Agencies," finds that a majority of board members in fifteen cities denied that outside groups had particular influence.

81. Mogoluf, "A Developmental Approach," would say that strong public
agency influence indicates EYOA is still in the first of two stages of community
action program development. In the first stage the primary concern is self-
maintenance and this requires serving the interests of other organizations. In the
second stage the action programs have enough support to push for institutional
change.

82. It is paradoxical that agency people often imply that riots are the work of
agitators and that community people often say the war on poverty is the work of
the joint powers. Agency people are quick to deny that they have the power attributed to them, but they are not as quick to question their own realism in attribut-
ing so much power to agitators.

83. *Los Angeles Times* article, August 5, 1968, Goe testified before a City
Council committee that the mayor's office took the initiative in creating EYOA.

84. For example, the mayor was concerned that Congressman Hawkins not
get control of EYOA. Another example is that the representatives successfully
prevented critical comments about the public agencies from being included in any
EYOA resolutions.

85. See chapter 2.

86. When a proposal for extending the Saugus Camp came before the board
at the end of the summer, five community representatives voted against it, and
since only seventeen members were present at the meeting the proposal failed.
There was stunned silence in the room, then agency representatives bustled about
and succeeded in getting the five to change their votes by making symbolic
modifications.

87. See citations in chapter 2. After the resignation of the first executive director signs appeared that the city's relative position might be changing. The five-
man committee appointed by the chairman to select the new director included a
county man but no city man. This led to vigorous protests from the city. The
chairman's official response was that the community representatives from city
districts are representatives of the city because technically the city designates the
representatives. (This view is in marked contrast with the previous determination
on the part of agency representatives to avoid any connection with the choice of
community representatives. Their claim was that city designation was a formality,
merely confirming the election results.) Actually the chairman seemed determined
to prevent the city from having as much influence over the board as it had had in
the past.

88. Marris and Rein, *Dilemmas of Social Reform*, p. 154, and Banfield, *Big
City Politics*, p. 92. The Senate Subcommittee report, *Examination of the War on
Poverty*, 1967, suggests that community action programs are most effective where
a governing coalition, with notably strong leadership from the mayor, supports them
and makes institutional change possible. See Vol. III, p. 799, and Vol. IV, p. 902.
But it is debatable whether the support of the mayor and the coalition of public
agencies in Los Angeles has constituted strong leadership for institutional change,
The next chapter presents examples of institutional change which have occurred,
but the argument here is that the governing coalition has used EYOA for its own
interests and these do not involve initiating institutional change as much as having
a scapegoat.

89. See Hunter, *Community Power Structure*.

90. Dahl, *Who Governs?*

91. Bachrach and Baratz, "Two Faces of Power," pp. 947–952. See Merelman,
"On the Neo-Elitist Critique of Community Power," pp. 451–460, for a critique of
Bachrach and Baratz's neo-elitist view of community power and the resulting ex-
change of letters in *American Political Science Review,* December 1968.

92. This influence has been maintained without resort to a provision in the

Joint Powers Agreement which requires that the prevailing vote on any action must include votes cast by "at least one member from each of three signatory parties." Even though there have been prevailing votes that did not meet this requirement the losing side never felt the need to raise this issue because they had other ways to protect their interests. Yet at least some of the joint powers representatives knew that the provision was available and referred to it as their secret weapon. The requirement serves as a formal indication of the fact that the joint powers have a veto if they want to use it. In 1970 this requirement was criticized by OEO as a violation of guidelines.

93. See *Los Angeles Times*, August 23, 1968, for the director's comments that the public agencies have cooperated with EYOA and his awareness of the charge that he is a tool of the establishment.

94. See Merelman's letter in *American Political Science Review*, December 1968, p. 1299.

95. Bachrach and Baratz, *Power and Poverty*, develops this idea more freely.

96. See Greer, *Urban Renewal and American Cities*. Selznick, *TVA and the Grass Roots*, p. 264, correctly points out that it is naïve to suppose that there is anything inherently bad in this.

97. See Marris and Rein, *Dilemmas of Social Reform*, p. 169; Crain, *Politics of School Desegregation*, chapters 13 and 21.

98. Barber, in *Power in Committees*, has a chapter on the differences between committee members' generalizations about the power structure and their operating assumptions. This discrepancy appears to exist among EYOA board members. Observation suggests that even public agency representatives who denied that any groups control the board were very careful not to antagonize certain other public agencies on the board.

99. This bypassing of board members is a source of irritation to some of them.

100. Selznick, *TVA and the Grass Roots*, p. 259.

101. *Ibid.*, pp. 231–237.

102. Cloward, "The War on Poverty: Are the Poor Kept out?", p. 56.

103. Statement in Senate Subcommittee, *Examination of the War on Poverty Hearings*, 1967, Part I, p. 290.

104. And more actively than those studied by Brandeis University, "Board Members of Community Action Agencies."

105. The audience for meetings usually is around twenty-five, but for funding sessions it goes as high as one hundred.

106. Scoble, "Negro Politics," p. 36, points out that Negro leadership in Los Angeles is specialized. Poverty is only one policy arena and it has been the concern primarily of Congressman Hawkins and Opal Jones. But even these two have not been active in fighting EYOA since 1966. Gittel, *Participants and Participation*, presents a typology of participation in school policy formulation: (1) closed—only professionals in the system participate; (2) limited—specialized educational interest groups also participate; and (3) open—groups not wholly concerned with education participate. Participation in EYOA policy would clearly be in the second, or limited category.

107. This parallels the feeling expressed by many EYOA staff and board members—see chapter 2.

108. In other cities, such as New York and San Francisco, such groups did develop, but national as well as local pressures are increasingly working against them. See Krosney, *Beyond Welfare*, on the retreat in New York.

CHAPTER 5

1. Moore, *Social Change*, pp. 16, 20.

2. Several recent studies stress the importance of the attitudes of board mem-

NOTES TO PP. *81–84*

bers for an explanation of the action the boards take. Wilson, ed., *City Politics and Public Policy*, p. 266, and Crain *et al.*, *The Politics of School Desegregation*. An interest in attitudes should not be equated with a belief that change must wait until attitudes change. On the contrary, the position here is that change in structure may lead to changes in attitude which are conducive to further changes in structure.

3. For references to the literature on the impact of participation in groups on political attitudes see Milbrath, *Political Participation*, and Lane, *Political Life: Why and How People Get Involved in Politics*.

4. References to the literature on adult socialization can be found in Brim and Wheeler, *Socialization after Childhood*; Clausen, "Recent Developments in Socialization Theory and Research," pp. 139–155; Clausen, ed., *Socialization and Society*; Jennings and Niemi, "The Transmission of Political Values from Parent to Child," pp. 169–184; Rose, *Human Behavior and Social Processes*; Berg, "Adult Socialization and Social Work Practice," pp. 89–94; Dawson and Prewitt, *Political Socialization*.

5. See Brim, *Socialization after Childhood*, pp. 90, 113; Jennings and Niemi, "Transmission of Political Values," p. 183.

6. See Milbrath's stimulus-organism-response model in *Political Participation*.

7. Bauer, de Sola Pool, and Dexter (chapter 10) found that role more than background determined what the businessmen learned; *American Business and Public Policy*.

8. Fred Greenstein, "The Impact of Personality on Politics: An Attempt To Clear Away Underbrush," pp. 629–641.

9. Eleven agency representatives said that the community representatives had had influence and five gave negative responses. Note that when agency representatives were asked to name influential board members, only seven made even qualified mention of community representatives. And in spite of the previously mentioned awareness by the community representatives that the public agency representatives have predominant influence, five community representatives said that community representatives had influenced the board and only two said they had not.

10. This finding supports Shostak's point that community representatives made many personal remarks on the Philadelphia board; "Promoting Participation for the Poor."

11. Shostak also found that Philadelphia representatives called attention to the weak aspects of projects. *Ibid.*

12. No one said it explicitly but they implied that the presence of community representatives was inhibiting to the agency representatives. They could not talk about poverty the way they would around agency people. It has been suggested that this parallels the feelings of faculty members at faculty meetings when students are present.

13. These comments parallel Shostak's findings in "Promoting Participation of the Poor." Three agency representatives specifically pointed out that negative influences on the board did not come solely from community representatives. They said that agency people also had hang-ups, prolonged meetings by unnecessary talk, and were inconsistent. Observation confirms strikingly parallel behavior between the agency and community representatives. For example, both types walked out of meetings after resigning in the face of perceived insults. Both got angry when told to put their complaints in writing, and when questioned in public both interrupted others, and when interrupted demanded that the other person "wait until I'm finished." Both charged others with being inconsistent yet were unaware of their own inconsistencies. Both were openly rude to other board members (often bringing gasps from "indigenous" onlookers). Few seemed aware of the paradox that when someone from his own agency did x, it was understandable, but when a community representative did x, it was seen as a "hang-up."

14. In the interview the community representatives tended to stress the positive examples of influence to justify their performance, but they also were quick to qualify their remarks.

15. Rossi and Dentler, *Politics of Urban Renewal*, p. 152.

16. Of course it is not possible to determine whether or not those decisions would have been made without the efforts of the community representatives. Shostak in Philadelphia also found that community representatives pushed for more jobs in the poverty programs for indigenous people and for revisions in programs. "Promoting Participation of the Poor," p. 620.

17. Kramer, *Participation of the Poor*, p. 245, also argues that poverty representation is useful even when policy outcomes are not significantly influenced. See also Mogulof, "Citizen Participation: The Local Perspective," p. 122.

18. Contrast this proportion with *Intergovernmental Relations in the Poverty Program*, which found that 142 community action program directors felt representatives had been useful especially in pointing out needs, and only three said representatives had not been useful.

19. Note how these types of contributions parallel the agency members' concepts of the representational role of the community members. All the agency representatives would undoubtedly agree that there is a need for public relations and for communications about the attitudes in the community. The argument would be over whether or not community representation on the board is the best way to fulfill this function. For example, the respondent most opposed to community representatives being on the board expressed approval for the idea of having an advisory council of community people. Others opposed this idea because it would not build community confidence but instead would increase community frustration.

20. Ten agency representatives are classified as positive, 7 negative; 3 community representatives positive, 5 negative; thus percentages are 50 percent positive for agency representatives and 37.5 percent for community representatives. But a change in the expressed attitude of just one person in either group, namely one community representative being classified as positive rather than negative, and one agency representative being classified as negative rather than positive, would make the proportions quite close.

21. Rein, "Community Action Programs," similarly describes community action programs as funnels "unable to insist on either innovation or coordination as a precondition for receipt of funds" and unable to ensure compliance.

22. This kind of rallying of support for EYOA was seen when the state tried to use the Green amendment to declare itself the CAA for all of California. In response, individuals such as Supervisor Hahn, who had opposed EYOA, praised it publicly as better, even with all its faults, than the state would be.

23. Brandeis University, "Board Members of Community Action Agencies," also found that community representatives tended to feel that CAAs had not been sufficiently responsive to the needs of the poor.

24. Contrast this with the positive attitudes among Negroes toward the war on poverty in 1965 when it was just starting, as reported by Sears, "Political Attitudes of Los Angeles Negroes," p. 11. He found that 42 percent felt the war on poverty helped a lot; 45 percent said it helped a little; 7 percent said it had no effect.

25. Four subjects either did not respond or gave responses that were not clearly either positive or negative. No one specifically mentioned positive feelings for the staff and negative feelings for the executive director. There was one mention of positive feelings for the staff and a tendency to question their recommendations nevertheless.

26. For similar criticisms of the Boston CAA staff see Thernstrom, *Poverty, Planning, and Politics*, p. 114.

27. Five hostile to EYOA, only three hostile to staff.

28. Grodzins, in Elazar, ed., *The American System: A New View of Government in the United States*. Local officials involved in EYOA were much more hostile to the federal agencies than one might expect from the study of the Senate Subcommittee on Intergovernmental Relations. U.S. Congress, Senate Subcommittee on Intergovernmental Relations, *The Federal System as Seen by State and Local Officials*.

29. See supporting comments by the executive director, *Los Angeles Times*, August 23, 1968, in an article by Jack Jones, "Poverty War Director Assesses 4½ Year Fight." The mayor of Detroit gave a detailed list of the effect of CAAs on city government; Senate Subcommittee, *Examination of the War on Poverty, Hearings*, 1967, Part I, p. 107. See also Kramer, *Participation of the Poor*, pp. 239–247.

30. This institutional change has been stimulated by CAAs throughout the country. See Senate Subcommittee, *Examination of the War on Poverty*, 1967, IV, 914.

31. For a list of agency failures to change, see Senate Subcommittee, *Examination of the War on Poverty*, 1967, IV, 913.

32. Marris and Rein, *Dilemmas of Social Reform*, pp. 222–223.

33. *Ibid.*, p. 168; *Yale Law Journal*, "Participation of the Poor," p. 620; Shostak, "Promoting Participation for the Poor," p. 68.

34. The difficulties inherent in studies of change have led social scientists to do static studies. See Matthews, *U.S. Senators*, and Milbrath, *Political Participation*. But new emphasis is being put on questions of change. See Coser, *The Functions of Social Conflict*; Dahrendorf, *Class and Class Conflict in Industrial Society*; Coleman, *Community Conflict*; Moore, *Social Change*.

35. See chapter 5.

36. In the following analysis the numbers do not always add up to 17 agency representatives or 8 community representatives because respondents were not included when they gave no response or responses that were not clearly either positive or negative.

37. The responses may be misleading because no definition was given of what was meant by militancy. The question reveals word associations that could be used as a start for further clarification.

38. Contrast this with Huckshorn's study of Los Angeles councilmen, "Spotlight on City Councilmen," which found that the odds were two to one in favor of Republicans. As would be expected, there was a high correlation between the agency representatives' statements about their parents' party identification and their own party identification. To the extent that these are indications of differences, they favor the Democrats; four agency representatives who are Democrats said their parents were either both Republicans, or one Republican and one Democrat.

39. See Marris and Rein, *Dilemmas of Social Reform*, pp. 202–223, for comments on professional reformers.

40. In spite of the fact that the reasons for that evaluation may differ within the group.

41. Dawson and Prewitt, *Political Socialization*, p. 24.

42. Only two agency people maintained that the community representatives had not changed much and these two people were new members of the board, having come on approximately a year after the community representatives. There was no response from three; they were not asked specifically about changes in community representatives and did not mention any in response to a general question about how other board members had changed.

43. This parallels the findings of the Senate Subcommittee, *Examination of the War on Poverty*, 1967, IV, 908. Representatives at first did not understand the proceedings but gradually they became more expressive and forceful.

44. Several community representatives stressed that committee meetings were where they learned the most.

45. Small group literature sometimes implies that participation always leads to understanding. Verba, in *Small Groups and Political Behavior*, points out that participation may lead to hostility. See also the literature on unequal status contact and prejudice, for example: Allport, *The Nature of Prejudice*, chapter 16; Simpson and Yinger, "The Sociology of Race and Ethnic Relations" in Mertons, Broom, and Cottrell, eds., *Sociology Today*; Simpson and Yinger, *Racial and Cultural Minorities*; Newcomb, "The Study of Concensus" in Merton, Broom, and Cottrell, eds., *Sociology Today*; Festinger and Kelley, *Changing Attitudes through Social Contact*.

46. The terms "establishment-oriented," "downtown-oriented," "copping out," "being won over," "selling out," and "Uncle Tom" are used throughout as rough equivalents. Their meaning is imprecise, reflecting a feeling on the part of the user that the individual is sympathetic to or a supporter of the powerful people, whoever "they" are.

47. Even though at other times the community representatives referred to EYOA as "we."

48. And even the community representatives who did talk about a more positive attitude toward the program indicated only partial satisfaction with it, one saying, "I don't say I accept it—how things work—because we're working to change a lot of things, but at least you know why things work the way they do."

49. By contrast, Sears, in "Political Attitudes of Los Angeles Negroes," found curfew area residents generally trustful toward local government, both the city and county. But he points out that respondents had little information (about 13 percent had no opinion). And there were large areas of disaffection, especially toward Mayor Yorty.

50. The interview originally was designed to elicit feelings about the county and the voluntary agencies but answers from the community representatives did not reveal distinct attitudes toward the county or the voluntary agencies.

51. See Almond and Verba, *The Civic Culture*, and Milbrath, *Political Participation*.

52. This did not provide useful distinctions among agency representatives because they responded from the perspective of "people on the top," (for example, "there is no monolithic power structure in Los Angeles, no single person with a preponderance of power").

53. Contrast this with Bayes, *Political Participation and Geographic Mobility*, p. 116, who finds Los Angeles respondents indicated a greater orientation toward national than local. Sears, "Political Attitudes of Los Angeles Negroes," p. 22, reports similar findings in the curfew area.

54. Sears, "Political Attitudes of Los Angeles Negroes," p. 17.

55. Scoble, "Negro Politics in Los Angeles," comments on the increase in militant styles of leadership.

56. Wilson, *Negro Politics: The Search for Leadership*. Scoble, "Negro Politics in Los Angeles," p. 24. See also Shostak, "Promoting Participation for the Poor," p. 70.

57. White, in "Articulateness, Political Mobility, and Conservatism," found a higher percentage of Republicans. On EYOA the Republican described himself as a moderate Republican and gave some idiosyncratic reasons for switching party identification in 1962 from Democrat to Republican to work in a specific election to defeat an entrenched Democratic incumbent. Then in 1964 he voted for Goldwater on the grounds he was better qualified to end the war in Vietnam.

58. Agency representatives were merely asked to list their organizational affiliations on the questionnaire; no attempt was made to get at changes in organi-

zational participation or in political participation because it was assumed that the agency representatives already had high rates of participation which could not be significantly changed by EYOA membership.

59. The exception was the person whose board experience contributed to his increased hostility and the increased disorganization of his personal life, and even this person states an intention to be active once his life stabilizes.

60. *Inter-Governmental Relations in the Poverty Program*, section 3, reports that eighty-six executive directors said yes, community action programs had increased activity of the poor; eighty-four said no.

61. A *Los Angeles Times* article on what happened to the seven interim community representatives after they left the board supports this generalization. Over half of them made significantly more than $4,000 and worked in poverty-related programs. Paul Weeks, "Five Earn Too Much To Sit on Poverty Board Today," January 16, 1967. White, "Articulateness, Political Mobility, and Conservation," p. 15, also reports that the Philadelphia community representatives obtained jobs in the poverty program.

62. See Pearl and Riessman, *New Careers for the Poor.*

63. Dawson and Prewitt, *Political Socialization*, p. 24.

64. Brim, *Socialization after Childhood*, pp. 45–56.

CHAPTER 6

1. Arrangements for the original interviews were made in person with three of the representatives when they were at the EYOA office checking on election results. The others were contacted by phone and had never seen the interviewer until she appeared at their doors. All of them had only her word as to her credentials.

2. Several agency and staff people at first felt the representatives were more informed than the original representatives, but later this opinion changed.

3. Five agency representatives said their first impression was that the new group was less hostile than the original group. One described them as a group of Uncle Toms "eagerly trying to find out what it is they should do to be good guys."

4. The community representatives had only vague impressions of what the city government was. In most cases they needed clarification of what was meant by the question.

5. Bowen and Massotti, "Spokesmen for the Poor," also found their poverty candidates lower on the scale of efficacy than they had expected.

6. This parallels Bowen and Masotti's comments on p. 104, "Spokesmen for the Poor."

7. Lane, *Political Ideology: Why the American Common Man Believes as He Does*, chapter 10.

8. In this they reflect the criticism prevalent in minority communities reported by the Koerner Commission in *Report of the National Advisory Commission on Civil Disorders.*

9. This finding contrasts with White's findings in "Articulateness, Political Mobility, and Conservatism," that the elected poor in Philadelphia were allegiants.

10. Almond and Verba, *The Civic Culture*, pp. 274–283.

11. And two of these three did not participate in any organizations after leaving school until they got involved in poverty organizations.

12. See Lane, *Political Life*, pp. 147–155, for a discussion of the relation of ego strength to participation. Note that the community representatives showed subjective feelings of personal efficacy. No objective assessment of their ego strength is attempted here.

13. They often asked the interviewer's impression since they knew all the new representatives were being interviewed.

14. Throughout the following discussion of changes, note will be made if the researcher's observations contradict the subjective reports; the absence of comment indicates that the subjective reports are consistent with observations.

15. Three representatives did not indicate increases in confidence. The explanation of one case is apparently that he had a high level of confidence before being on the board and the board did not increase or decrease the preexisting level of confidence. But the cases of the two other new community representatives are a source of speculation. Their experiences on the board seemed to increase their frustration and decrease their sense of confidence. In other words, it shook their preexisting feeling of worth. It would be interesting to find out whether this phenomena persists at the end of their three-year term or whether it merely reflects temporary feelings of discouragement such as those reported by the original representatives who nevertheless felt increased confidence by the end of their term.

16. Three of these were classified as negative toward EYOA in the first interviews, but review of the transcripts confirms that they became more hostile.

17. The remaining representative felt the whole board was being used by specific community organizations in one geographic area of Los Angeles. The three representatives who felt positive toward EYOA indicated that the main pressures on them came from staffs of delegate agencies and the people involved with those agencies.

18. It may also explain why some agency representatives saw them as less hostile than the original group.

19. It would be interesting to see if the large positive response is still present at the ends of their terms, or whether the apparent difference between the two groups of community representatives is attributable to the new community representatives still being close to the board. This closeness may mean they give more weight to their favorable feelings toward specific individuals than to their generalized picture, which tends to be more negative.

20. The remaining community representative showed so much ambivalence that classification was difficult. He felt more negative about his own influence on EYOA but more positive about his influence on other agencies.

21. Almond and Verba, in *The Civic Culture*, say that reference to this strategy of influence is more prevalent in the United States than in the other countries they studied (pp. 145–159).

22. The community representatives' underlying mistrust of officials in spite of overlays of positive feelings was underscored by their immediate response to the assassination of Robert Kennedy. They assumed that it, like the previous assassination of President Kennedy, was a conspiracy by the establishment to kill people sympathetic to the poor.

23. One had become slightly more negative, saying that Washington is not listening to the poor people because they, the poor, do not have the money for lobbyists.

24. This difference may be primarily an artifact of the different research strategies used. The new representatives tended to understate the changes in their answers about individual influence, and the magnitude of the change only became apparent in comparison with the original interviews. Greater familiarity with the second community representatives also made it possible to do more probing in the second interview.

25. The new representatives, like the old ones, did not indicate any increase in involvement in politics.

26. A year and a half later the pressures had escalated; representatives talked of physical intimidation and seemed just as upset as the original community representatives had been.

27. Lane, *Political Ideology*, chapter 4, describes the techniques his subjects

used to account for their own status. Their claims of moral equality are similar to those made by the community representatives.

28. "Spokesmen for the Poor." See also Scoble, "Poverty and/or Politics," p. 8, which reports that the poor tend to identify themselves as working class and lack class consciousness. Elinson, *Folk Politics*, pp. 115–118, gives an interesting description of how working class men avoid giving the answers to questions of class which social scientists think they should.

29. White, in "Articulateness, Political Mobility, and Conservatism," p. 13, also found that poverty candidates made an effort to distinguish themselves from other poor people. Elinson, *Folk Politics*, p. 53, and Lane, *Political Ideology*, pp. 71–72, comment on the lack of sympathy of working class men for welfare recipients. And Scott Briar, "Welfare from Below: Recipients' Views of the Public Welfare System," in Tenbroek, ed., *The Law of the Poor*, p. 51, finds that welfare recipients have negative impressions of other people on welfare.

30. The fact that two of the three described themselves as lower class (the only two community representatives to do so) need not ncessarily be taken as indicating a class position lower than that of the other representatives, but may indicate rather that they see themselves as low when compared with what they hope to become. They are using a different standard of comparison.

31. OEO originally opposed paying representatives but later modifications were made. See Senate, *Expand the War on Poverty Hearings*, 1965, pp. 89–90. *Yale Law Journal*, "Participation of the Poor," p. 620, reports that in Philadelphia the representatives were mainly interested in getting jobs for themselves.

32. This finding supports Riessman's view that membership on boards can develop new leaders. Riessman, "Anti-Poverty Programs and the Role of the Poor," in Gordon, ed., *Poverty in America*.

33. See Scoble, "Social Mobility and Political Leadership: A Research Note," pp. 17, 18, for a discussion of literature relevant to the problem of overconformity and possible differences between the phenomenon in leaders and nonleaders.

34. White, "Articulateness, Political Mobility, and Conservatism," argues the opposite.

35. This would support Thompson's findings for nonleaders as reported in Scoble's paper "Social Mobility."

36. See Schlesinger's use of careers to explain behavior in *Ambition and Politics*. See also Levinson's typology of nonprofessionals based on career aspirations. Levinson and Schiller, "Role Analysis of the Indigenous Nonprofessional," pp. 95–101.

37. The committee structure helped create the outcast feeling because the same four community representatives were members of the two committees that met most often in the first months.

38. The leaders did not show marked changes in their prior evaluations of EYOA or in their styles; one was positive toward EYOA, one negative; one was militant, one moderate; the changes were mainly in the areas of confidence and image.

CHAPTER 7

1. See Agger *et al., The Rulers and the Ruled*, pp. 51–58, for the distinction between power and access.

2. Almond and Verba, *The Civic Culture*.

3. Liebow, *Tally's Corner: A Study of Negro Streetcorner Men*.

4. *Dilemmas of Social Reform*, p. 168; "Reformers, Machines, and the War on Poverty"; *TVA and the Grass Roots*. See also Kramer, *Participation of the Poor*,

p. 257; Brandeis University, "Community Representation in Community Action Programs," p. 22; and Peterson, "Forms of Representation." Contradictory findings are reported in Mogulof, "Citizen Participation: The Local Perspective," pp. 65 and 80.

5. Mogulof, in "Citizen Participation: The Local Perspective," says that the parties that were formerly merely the subject of negotiation have become participants in the negotiations, p. 122.

6. Bachrach and Baratz, "Two Faces of Power."

7. This view, which contrasts with the Parsonian stress on functional coordination, is developed in Dahrendorf's *Class and Class Conflict in Industrial Society.*

8. *Report of the National Advisory Commission on Civil Disorders.*

9. Kramer, *Participation of the Poor,* pp. 248–258, stresses socialization of minorities as an important outcome of CAAs.

10. Los Angeles does not fit easily into Greenstone and Peterson's scheme relating dispersion of power directly to the degree of reform in cities; "Reformers, Machines, and the War on Poverty."

11. *Ibid.* See also Thernstrom, *Poverty, Planning and Politics.*

12. Brandeis University, "Community Representation in Community Action Programs," finds that differences in CAAs "are associated systematically with differences between the cities in which the CAAs are located," p. 15.

13. Kramer, *Participation of the Poor,* pp. 245, 248–258; Mogulof, "Citizen Participation: The Local Perspective," p. 48.

14. Mogulof, "Citizen Participation: The Local Perspective."

15. Elazar, *American Federalism: A View from the States,* p. 81.

16. See *Intergovernmental Relations in the Poverty Program,* pp. 52–55.

17. Krosney, *Beyond Welfare,* pp. 15–16.

18. *Dilemmas of Social Reform,* p. 220.

19. *Ibid.* See also Kramer, *Participation of the Poor,* pp. 269–273. This conflict idea directly challenges the consensus view of social action which Rossi and Dentler, *Politics of Urban Renewal,* p. 107, describe in Chicago.

20. In 1969 there was federal pressure on EYOA to force both courses of action, but area councils still were not in operation by 1970, even though plans were being developed as they had been off and on since the beginning of the agency.

21. Some of the most obvious difficulties involve deciding on the number and location of area councils (which is complicated by the problem of whether they should relate to the existing electoral districts), what powers they should have, and how they should be staffed and financed. Problems also involve how the councils will select their community representative, either in a general election or from their own membership, or if there are more than eight councils how will they combine for the election of only eight representatives? Certainly the charade of having the representatives cover the whole EYOA area should be ended; instead they should represent the poverty pockets, however designated, and if people are still worried about the 53 percent of the population not in those pockets, there could be one at-large representative.

22. See Hawkins' suggestion for training with stipends in Senate Subcommittee, *Examination of the War on Poverty, Hearings,* 1967, part 12, p. 3760. See also Mogulof, "Citizen Participation: The Local Perspective," pp. 68–71.

23. OEO has stopped contracting with CAAs for research in order to ensure more independence, and this is also the trend in training CAA staffs.

24. What type of training would be most effective for community representatives is a question that individuals interested in various training approaches might give more attention to. One wonders about the impact of sensitivity training and group dynamics approaches that stress understanding and cooperation on political

groups in which there is a struggle for power. "Understanding" is not neutral; it may effect outcomes. See Killian, *Racial Crisis in America,* and Rossi and Dentler, *Politics of Urban Renewal,* p. 107.

25. Reference is often made to the Brown Act as another reason why such self-evaluation sessions are not possible.

26. In 1969 each community representative did get an office and a secretary in his district. Demands from the representatives for such offices gave certain staff members the support they needed to implement the plans which they had favored unsuccessfully in the past. Mogulof argues the importance of monetary support for representatives, "Citizen Participation: The Local Perspective," p. 61.

27. By 1969 the attempt at unity has been delivered a fearsome blow by a black-brown split among the representatives, a split much more severe than any previous one among the representatives.

BIBLIOGRAPHY
★ ★ ★ ★ ★ ★ ★

Bibliography

Abrahams, Marvin. "Functioning of Boards and Commissions in the Los Angeles City Government." Unpublished doctoral dissertation, University of California, Los Angeles, 1967.

Agger, P. E., D. Goldrich, and B. E. Swanson. *The Rulers and the Ruled.* New York: John Wiley and Sons, 1964.

Allport, Gordon. *The Nature of Prejudice.* New York: Anchor Books, 1958.

Almond, Gabriel, and S. Verba. *The Civic Culture: Political Attitudes and Democracy in Five Nations.* Boston: Little, Brown, 1963.

American Arbitration Association. "Study of CAP Elections." Mimeographed.

Bachrach, Peter. *The Theory of Democratic Elitism: A Critique.* Boston: Little, Brown, 1967.

Bachrach, Peter, and Morton Baratz. *Power and Poverty: Theory and Practice.* New York: Oxford University Press, 1970.

————. "Two Faces of Power," *American Political Science Review,* LVI (December 1962), 947–952.

Banfield, Edward. *Big City Politics.* New York: Random House, 1965.

————. *Political Influence.* New York: Free Press, 1961.

Banfield, Edward, and J. Q. Wilson. *City Politics.* New York: Vintage Books, 1963.

Barber, James David. *Power in Committees.* Chicago: Rand McNally, 1966.

Bauer, Raymond, Ithiel de Sola Pool, and Lewis A. Dexter. *American Business and Public Policy.* New York: Atherton Press, 1963.

Bayes, Jane. "Political Participation and Geographic Mobility in Los Angeles County, 1965." Unpublished doctoral dissertation, University of California, Los Angeles, 1967.

Becker, Howard, and B. Geer. "Participant Observation and Interviewing: A Comparison," *Human Organization,* XVI (Fall 1957), 28–32.

Berg, Philip. "Adult Socialization and Social Work Practice," *Social Work,* XII (April 1961), 89–94.

Bibby, John Franklin, and R. H. Davidson. *On Capitol Hill.* New York: Holt, Rinehart and Winston, 1967.

Blake, Aldrich. *You Wear the Big Shoe.* n.p., 1945.

Bollens, John. "Youth Opportunities Board of Greater Los Angeles: An Intergovernmental Approach to Youth and Other Problems." Mimeographed.

Bowen, Don R., and Louis H. Masotti. "Spokesmen for the Poor: An Analysis of Cleveland's Poverty Board Candidates," *Urban Affairs Quarterly*, IV (September 1968), 89–100.

Bowman, Lewis, and G. P. Boynton. "Recruitment Patterns among Local Party Officials: A Model and Some Preliminary Findings in Selected Locales," *American Political Science Review*, LX (September 1966), 667–676.

Brager, George A., and Francis P. Purcell, eds. *Community Action against Poverty*. New Haven: College and University Press, 1967.

Brandeis University. "Board Members of Community Action Agencies: An Analysis of Interview Data," Report no. 2. August 1968. Mimeographed.

————. "Community Representation in Community Action Programs," Report no. 5, March 1969. Mimeographed, OEO grant no. CG 68–9499 A 12.

Braybrooke, David, and Charles Lindblom. *A Strategy of Decision: Policy Evaluation as a Social Process*. New York: Free Press of Glencoe, 1963.

Briar, Scott. "Welfare from Below: Recipients Views of the Public Welfare System." In Jacobus Tenbroek, ed., *The Law of the Poor*. San Francisco: Chandler, 1966.

Brim, Orville, and Stanton Wheeler. *Socialization after Childhood*. New York: John Wiley and Sons, 1967.

Carney, Francis M., and John W. Reuss. "The Politics of the War on Poverty in Los Angeles." June 1967. Mimeographed draft.

Clausen, John A. "Recent Developments in Socialization Theory and Research," *Annals of the American Academy of Political and Social Science*, CCCLVII (May 1968), 139–155.

Clausen, John A., ed. *Socialization and Society*. Boston: Little, Brown and Co., 1968.

Cloward, Richard A. "The War on Poverty: Are the Poor Left Out?" *The Nation*, XXI (August 1965), 55–60.

Cohen, Nathan. "Los Angeles Riot Study: Summary and Implications for Policy." Institute of Government and Public Affairs, University of California, Los Angeles, June 1967.

Coleman, James. *Community Conflict*. New York: Free Press of Glencoe, 1957.

Coser, Lewis. *The Functions of Social Conflict*. New York: Free Press, 1956.

Crain, Robert L., *et al. The Politics of School Desegregation*. Chicago: Aldine Publ. Co., 1967.

Crouch, Winston, and Beatrice Dinerman. *Southern California Metropolis: A Study in the Development of Government for a Metropolitan Area*. Berkeley: University of California Press, 1964.

Dahl, Robert. *Who Governs?* New Haven: Yale University Press, 1961.

Dahrendorf, Ralph. *Class and Class Conflict in Industrial Society*. Stanford: Stanford University Press, 1959.

Davidson, Roger H. "Creative Federalism and the War on Poverty," *Poverty and Human Resources Abstract*, I (November-December 1966), 5–16.

Dawson, Richard, and Kenneth Prewitt, *Political Socialization*. Boston: Little, Brown, 1969.

Donovan, John. *The Politics of Poverty*. New York: Pegasus, 1967.

Downs, Anthony. *Inside Bureaucracy*. Boston: Little, Brown, 1967.

Economic and Youth Opportunity Agency. "The Board and the Administration: Their Roles, Expectations, and Relationships." Mimeographed.

Elazar, Daniel. *American Federalism: A View from the States.* New York: Crowell, 1966.

Elinson, Howard. *Folk Politics: The Political Mentality of White Working Class Voters.* New York: Basic Books, in press.

Etzioni, Amitai. *Modern Organizations.* Englewood Cliffs, N. J.: Prentic-Hall, 1964.

Evan, William M. "Dimensions of Participation in Voluntary Associations," *Social Forces,* XXXVI (December 1957), 48–153.

Fenno, Richard. "The Appropriations Committee as a Political System." In Robert Peabody, and Nelson Polsby, eds., *New Perspectives on the House of Representatives.* Chicago: Rand McNally, 1963.

Ferman, Louis, *et al.,* eds. *Poverty in America.* Ann Arbor: University of Michigan Press, 1965.

Festinger, Leon, and Harold Kelley. *Changing Attitudes through Social Contact.* Ann Arbor: University of Michigan Press, 1951.

Festinger, Leon, and Daniel Katz, eds. *Research Methods in the Behavioral Sciences.* New York: Dryden Press, 1953.

Freeman, Howard E., and Clarence C. Sherwood. "Research in Large-Scale Intervention Programs," *Journal of Social Issues,* XXI (January 1965), 11–28.

Gans, Herbert. *The Urban Villagers: Group and Class in the Life of Italian Americans.* New York: Free Press of Glencoe, 1962.

Gittel, Marilyn. *Participants and Participation.* New York: Frederick A. Praeger, 1967.

Gordon, Margaret S., ed. *Poverty in America.* San Francisco: Chandler, 1965.

Graham, Elinor. "The Politics of Poverty." In Ben Seligman, ed., *Poverty as a Public Issue.* New York: Free Press, 1965.

————. "Poverty and the Legislative Process." In Ben Seligman, ed., *Poverty as a Public Issue.* New York: Free Press, 1965.

Greenstein, Fred. "The Impact of Personality on Politics: An Attempt to Clear Away Underbrush," *American Political Science Review,* LXI (September 1967), 629–641.

Greenstone, J. David, and Paul E. Peterson. "Reformers, Machines, and the War on Poverty." In James Wilson, ed., *City Politics and Public Policy.* New York: John Wiley and Sons, 1968.

Greer, Scott. *Urban Renewal and American Cities: The Dilemma of Democratic Intervention.* Indianapolis: Bobbs Merrill, 1966.

Greer, Scott, and Peter Orleans. "Political Sociology." In Robert Faris, ed., *Handbook of Modern Sociology.* Chicago: Rand McNally, 1964.

Grodzins, Morton. In Daniel J. Elazar, ed., *The American System: A New View of Government in the United States.* Chicago: Rand McNally, 1966.

Gross, Neal, Ward Mason, and Alexander McEachern. *Explorations in Role Analysis: Studies of the School Superintendency Role.* New York: John Wiley and Sons, 1958.

Haddad, William F. "Mr. Shriver and the Savage Politics of Poverty," *Harper's Magazine,* CCXXXI (December 1965), 43–50.

Hare, A. Paul. "Interpersonal Relations in the Small Group." In Robert Faris, ed., *Handbook of Modern Sociology*. Chicago: Rand McNally, 1964.

Hauser, Philip, and Leo Schnore, eds. *The Study of Urbanization*. New York: John Wiley and Sons, 1965.

Hausknecht, Murray. "The Blue Collar Joiner." In Arthur Shostak and William Gomberg, eds., *Blue Collar World: Studies of the American Worker*. Englewood Cliffs, N. J.: Prentice-Hall, 1964.

Huckshorn, Robert J. "Spotlight on City Councilmen," *Bureau of Governmental Research Observer*. Los Angeles: Bureau of Governmental Research, University of California, 1957.

Hughes, Everett Cherrington. *Men and Their Work*. Glencoe, Ill.: Free Press, 1958.

Hunt, William H., Wilder W. Crane, and John Wahlke. "Interviewing Political Elites in Cross-Cultural Comparative Research," *American Journal of Sociology*, LXX (July 1964), 59–60.

Hunter, Floyd. *Community Power Structure: A Study of Decision Makers*. New York: Anchor Books, 1953.

Jaros, Dean, *et al.* "The Malevolent Leader: Political Socialization in an American Sub-culture," *American Political Science Review*, LXII (June 1968), 564–575.

Jennings, M. Kent, and Richard G. Niemi. "The Transmission of Politcal Values from Parent to Child," *American Political Science Review*, LXII (March 1968), 169–189.

Kahn, Robert, *et al. Organizational Stress: Studies in Role Conflict and Ambiguity*. New York: John Wiley and Sons, 1964.

Kain, John, and John Ries. "Congressmen, Incumbency, and Elections." Mimeographed.

Kammerer, Gladys, *et al. City Managers in Politics*. Gainesville: University of Florida, Social Science Monographs, 1962.

Keyserling, Leon. *Poverty and Deprivation in the United States*. Washington, D. C.: Conference on Economic Progress, 1962.

Killian, Lewis, and Charles Grigg. *Racial Crisis in America: Leadership in Conflict*. Englewood Cliffs, N. J.: Prentice-Hall, 1964.

Kramer, Ralph. *Participation of the Poor: Comparative Case Studies in the War on Poverty*. Englewood Cliffs, N. J.: Prentice-Hall, 1969.

Krosney, Herbert. *Beyond Welfare: Poverty in the Supercity*. New York: Holt, Rinehart and Winston, 1966.

Lane, Robert E. *Political Ideology: Why the American Common Man Believes What He Does*. New York: Free Press, 1962.

————. *Political Life: Why and How People Get Involved in Politics*. New York: Free Press, 1959.

Lee, Eugene. *The Politics of Nonpartisanship: A Study of California City Elections*. Berkeley: University of California Press, 1960.

Levinson, Perry, and Jeffry Schiller. "Role Analysis of the Indigenous Nonprofessional," *Social Work*, LXVII, no. 3 (July 1966), 95–101.

Levitan, S. "Planning the Anti-Poverty Strategy," *Poverty and Human Resources Abstract*, II (January–February 1967), 5–16.

Liebow, Elliot. *Tally's Corner: A Study of Negro Streetcorner Men*. Boston: Little, Brown, 1966.

Lipset, Seymour. *Political Man.* Garden City, N. Y.: Doubleday, 1960.

Lipset, Seymour, Martin Trow, and James Coleman. *Union Democracy.* New York: Anchor Books, 1956.

Los Angeles Times, January 16, 1967; May 8, 1967; October 27, 1967; April 5, 1968; June 17, 1968; August 5, 1968; August 23, 1968; September 9, 1968, and September 13, 1968.

Lurie, Ellen. "Community Action in East Harlem." In Leonard Duhl, ed., *The Urban Condition: People and Policy in the Metropolis.* New York and London: Basic Books, 1963.

Mailer, Norman. "The Steps of the Pentagon," *Harper's Magazine,* 45 (March 1968), 33–57.

Manley, John. "The House Committee on Ways and Means," *American Political Science Review,* LIX (December 1965), 927–939.

Marris, Peter, and Martin Rein. *Dilemmas of Social Reform: Poverty and Community Action in the U.S.* New York: Atherton Press, 1967.

Marshall, Dale. "War over Poverty: Politics of the Los Angeles Poverty Election." Mimeographed.

———. "Who Participates in What: A Bibliographic Essay on Individual Participation in Urban Areas," *Urban Affairs Quarterly,* IV (December 1968), 201–224.

Matthews, Donald. *U.S. Senators and Their World.* New York: Vintage Books, 1960.

Meeker, Marcia, and Lloyd Street. "Poverty Areas in Los Angeles County." Research Department, Welfare Planning Council, Los Angeles Region. Working Paper no. 51, April 1964.

Merelman, Richard M. "On the Neo-Elitist Critique of Community Power," *American Political Science Review,* LXII (June 1968), 451–460.

Meyerson, Martin, and Edward Banfield. *Politics, Planning, and the Public Interest.* New York: Free Press of Glencoe, 1955.

Michels, Robert. *Political Parties.* New York: Dover Press, 1959.

Milbrath, Lester. *Political Participation: How and Why Do People Get Involved in Politics?* Chicago: Rand McNally, 1965.

Miller, S. M. "The American Lower Classes: A Typological Approach." In Arthur Shostak, and William Gomberg, eds., *New Perspectives on Poverty.* Englewood Cliffs, N. J.: Prentice-Hall, 1965.

Mogulof, Melvin. "A Developmental Approach to the Community Action Program Idea," *Social Work,* XII, no. 2 (April 1967), 2–20.

———. "Citizen Participation: The Local Perspective." Mimeographed working paper, The Urban Institute, Washington, D. C., March 1970.

Moore, Wilbert. *Social Change.* Englewood Cliffs, N. J.: Prentice-Hall, 1963.

Moynihan, Daniel P. *Maximum Feasible Misunderstanding.* New York: Free Press, 1969.

———. "The Professors and the Poor," *Commentary,* XLVI (August 1968), 19–28.

———. "What Is Community Action?" *The Public Interest,* no. 5 (Fall 1966), 96.

Newcomb, T. M. "The Study of Consensus." In Robert Mertons, L. Broom, and L. C. Cottrell, eds., *Sociology Today.* New York: Basic Books, 1959.

New Republic. "When the Poor Are Powerless," CLIII (September 4, 1965), 7.

Olmsted, Michael. *The Small Group.* New York: Random House, 1959.

Ostrum, Vincent. "School Board Politics: An Analysis of Non-Partisanism in the Los Angeles City Board of Education." Unpublished Master's thesis, University of California, Los Angeles, 1945.

Pearl, Arthur, and Frank Riessman. *New Careers for the Poor: The Nonprofessional in Human Service.* New York: Free Press, 1965.

Peterson, Paul E. "Forms of Representation: Participation of the Poor in the Community Action Program, *American Political Science Review,* LXIV (June 1970), 491–507.

Rein, Martin. "Community Action Programs: A Critical Reassessment," *Resources Abstract,* III (May–June 1968), Supplement.

Riessman, Frank. "Anti-Poverty Programs and the Role of the Poor." In Margaret Gordon, ed., *Poverty in America.* San Francisco: Chandler, 1965.

Riessman, Frank, and Nathan Glazer. *Faces in the Crowd.* New Haven: Yale University Press, 1952.

Riessman, Frank, et al. *Mental Health of the Poor.* New York: Free Press, 1964.

Rose, Arnold. *Human Behavior and Social Processes: An Interactionist Approach.* Boston: Houghton Mifflin, 1962.

Rossi, Peter, and Robert Dentler. *The Politics of Urban Renewal: The Chicago Findings.* New York: Free Press of Glencoe, 1961.

Rubin, Lillian. "Maximum Feasible Participation: The Origins, Implications, and Present Status," *Poverty and Human Resources Abstract,* II (November–December 1967), 5–18.

Scheiber, Harry. *The Condition of American Federalism: An Historian's View.* Prepared for the Senate Subcommittee on Intergovernmental Relations. Washington, D.C.: U.S. Government Printing Office, 1966.

Schlesinger, Joseph. *Ambition and Politics: Political Careers in the United States.* Chicago: Rand McNally, 1966.

Schwartz, Morris, and Charlotte Schwartz. "Problems in Participant Observation," *American Journal of Sociology,* LX (January 1965), 343–353.

Scoble, Harry. "Interdisciplinary Perspectives on Poverty in America: The View from Political Science." Paper delivered at the Symposium on Interdisciplinary Perspectives on Poverty in America, University of Kentucky, April 1967.

———. "Negro Politics in Los Angeles: The Quest for Power." Los Angeles: University of California, Institute of Government and Public Affairs, 1967.

———. "Poverty and/of Politics." Paper prepared for the Panel on Social Change and the Poor of the American Psychological Association, San Francisco, Calif., September 1, 1968. Mimeographed.

———. "Social Mobility and Political Leadership: A Research Note." August 1968. Mimeographed.

Sears, David. "Political Attitudes of Los Angeles Negroes." Los Angeles: University of California, Institute of Government and Public Affairs, 1967.

Selznick, Philip. *TVA and the Grass Roots: A Study in the Sociology of Formal Organization.* Berkeley, University of California Press, 1949.

Shostak, Arthur. "Promoting Participation for the Poor," *Social Work*, XI (January 1966), 64–72.

Simpson, G. E., and J. M. Yinger. *Racial and Cultural Minorities*. New York: Harper, 1958.

———. "The Sociology of Race and Ethnic Relations." In R. K. Mertons, L. Broom, and L. S. Cottrell, eds., *Sociology Today*. New York: Basic Books, 1959.

Stringfellow, William. "Representation of the Poor in American Society," *Law and Contemporary Problems*, XXXI (Winter 1966), 142–151.

Thernstrom, Stephan. *Poverty, Planning, and Politics in the New Boston: Origins of the ABCD*. New York: Basic Books, 1969.

Town Hall, Los Angeles. Municipal and County Government Section. *A Study of the Los Angeles City Charter: A Report*, 1963.

U.S. Advisory Commission on Intergovernmental Relations. *Intergovernmental Relations in the Poverty Program: A Commission Report*. Washington, D. C.: Government Printing Office, 1966.

U.S. Congress. House. Committee on Education and Labor. *Economic Opportunity Act of 1964*. Hearings before the Subcommittee on the War on Poverty Programs, 88th Cong., 2d Sess., 1964.

———. *Antipoverty Programs in New York City and Los Angeles*. Hearings before the Subcommittee on the War on Poverty Programs, 89th Cong., 1st Sess., 1965.

———. *Examination of the War on Poverty Program*. Hearings before the Subcommittee on Poverty Programs, 89th Cong., 1st Sess., 1965.

———. *Economic Opportunity Act: Amendments of 1967*. Hearings before Special Ad Hoc Subcommittee, 90th Cong., 1st Sess., 1967.

———. *Congressional Record*. 90th Cong., 1st Sess., 1967.

U.S. Congress. Senate. Committee on Labor and Public Welfare. *Expand the War on Poverty*. Hearings before the Select Subcommittee on Poverty, 89th Cong., 1st Sess., 1965.

———. Subcommittee on Employment, Manpower, and Poverty of the Committee on Labor and Public Welfare. *Examination of the War on Poverty*. 90th Cong., 1st Sess., 1967.

———. *Examination of the War on Poverty: Staff and Consultant Reports*. 90th Con., 1st Sess., 1967.

———. Subcommittee on Intergovernmental Relations. *The Federal System as Seen by State and Local Officials*. Washington, D.C.: Government Printing Office, 1962.

———. *Congressional Record*. 90th Cong., 1st Sess., 1967.

U.S. National Advisory Commission on Civil Disorders. *Report of the National Advisory Commission on Civil Disorders*. Washington, D.C.: Government Printing Office, 1968.

U.S. Office of Economic Opportunity. Community Action Program. *Community Action Program Guide*. Washington, D.C.: Government Printing Office, 1965.

———. Community Action Program memo of January 11, 1967.

———. *Organizing Communities for Action*. February 1968.

Verba, Sidney. *Small Groups and Political Behavior*. Princeton, N.J.: Princeton University Press, 1961.

Wahlke, John, Heinz Eulau, *et al. The Legislative System: Explorations in Legislative Behavior.* New York: John Wiley and Sons, 1962.

Walker, Jack L. "A Critique of the Elitist Theory of Democracy," *American Political Science Review,* XL (June 1966), 285–295.

Warner, W. Lloyd, Paul P. Van Riper, Norman H. Martin, and Orvis F. Collins. *The American Federal Executive.* New Haven: Yale University Press, 1963.

Weber, Max. In H. H. Gerth and C. W. Mills, eds. *From Max Weber: Essays in Sociology.* New York: Oxford University Press, 1946.

White, Elliot. "Articulateness, Political Mobility, and Conservatism: An Analysis of the Philadelphia Anti-Poverty Election." Mimeographed.

Wilson, James Q. *The Amateur Democrat.* Chicago: University of Chicago Press, 1962.

Wilson, James Q., ed. *City Politics and Public Policy.* New York: John Wiley and Sons, 1968.

———. "A Guide to Reagan Country: The Political Culture of Southern California." *Commentary,* XLIII (May 1967), 37–45.

———. *Negro Politics: The Search for Leadership.* New York: Free Press, 1960.

Yablonsky, Lewis. *The Hippie Trip.* New York: Pegasus, 1968.

Yale Law Journal. "Participation of the Poor," LXXV (March 1966), 599–629.

Yankelovich, Daniel, Inc. *Study of the Effects of Sections 210 and 211 of the 1967 Amendments to the Economic Opportunity Amendments.* Volume I, February 1969, Contract with OEO.

Index